Steven E

.irector of Public Psychiatry

Judith _____ ine

.ll-time writer and editor with the International Longevity Center,
and a former editor with Quality Paperback Book Club.

have been married for 14 years and have faced many of the issues
challenges they write about in *Midlife*. They live in New York City.

Midlife
A MANUAL

STEVEN ESTRINE, PH.D.
JUDITH ESTRINE

ELEMENT
Boston, Massachusetts • Shaftesbury, Dorset

Melbourne, Victoria

Text design and cover design © Element Books, Inc. 1999
Text © Steven and Judith Estrine 1999

First published in the USA in 1999 by
Element Books, Inc.
160 North Washington Street,
Boston, Massachusetts 02114

Published in Great Britain in 1999 by
Element Books Limited
Shaftesbury, Dorset SP7 8BP

Published in Australia in 1999 by
Element Books Limited for
Penguin Books Australia Limited
487 Maroondah Highway, Ringwood, Victoria 3134

Library of Congress Cataloging-in-Publication data available

British Library Cataloguing in Publication data available

Printed and bound in the United States by Edwards Brothers

ISBN 1-86204-690-5

Dedication

In memory of Frank and Adele Estrine
and
Jacob and Molly Menschenfreund

Table of Contents

Acknowledgements

We are very grateful to our friends and family members, who put up with late night phone interviews and intrusions upon their privacy with forbearance and good humor. We believe we've included everyone who participated, but if we left anyone out, please understand that it was unintentional.

For allowing us to tell their stories we thank:

Gail Albert, Shelley Ballad, Shellie Berman, Joan Brady, John Brady, Linda Brady, Mark Chimsky, Delores Etrog, Carole Gordon, Donna Greenberg, Colga Hylton, Marilyn Kamile, Nancy Kelton, Gabe Koz, Nancy Lindenauer, Robert Lustig, Rita Moran, Nora O'Brien, Lorraine O'Brien, Aviva Rice, Israel Rice, Sharon Rosenberg, Steve Silverstein, Carol Stamaty.

Our thanks to the staff at Element: Roberta Scimone for having encouraged us from the beginning; Darren Kelly for his efficient and levelheaded advice; and Greg Brandenburgh for his sound editorial judgment.

Thanks to Lenny Emmerman, Donna Greenberg, Rita Moran, Alan Siegel and Laura Wood for their careful reading of an early draft and their insightful comments and suggestions; to Linda Leccese for transcribing a mountain of tapes with accuracy and speed; to Naomi Zimmelman for making us look good in a photograph; to Jeff and Nancy Lindenauer for being the project's godparents; to Robert Castillo for his technical support; to Aura Akhlaghi for working around the chaos; and to Yippy and Tiger for their quiet humor.

We thank our sisters, Charlotte Weinberger and Gail Menschenfreund for their love, support and great stories.

Finally, our heartfelt thanks to Amanda, who makes it all worthwhile.

How to Use
This Book

Midlife: A Manual is a practical guide to help you address some of the major challenges you experience in your midlife years. It describes a variety of issues, offers insights and suggestions about ways you might handle them, and presents the stories and observations of a variety of people in midlife who have gone through similar experiences. You'll see that there's more than one "right" way to resolve some of the tough issues with which you find yourself struggling. This book will help you find your own answers.

Although you may begin to identify with some of the people whose stories we tell—and perhaps dislike others—never forget that you're the real hero/heroine of this book. You are the subject of every chapter, and you stand in the center of every challenge.

If you're like most people, you don't give yourself enough credit for having matured and for knowing more than you think you do. That's why we've included self evaluation tests. The questions are designed to get you to think about your life—and yourself—in new ways. They are tools to help you understand who you are at this juncture in life, as compared to where you may have been ten years ago. They can also help you plan the road you'd like to take as the next phase of your life journey unfolds.

Introduction

Midlifers today are breaking all the rules. We are healthier and have longer life expectancies than at any other time in the history of the world. At the turn of the century, people could expect to live to be forty-two years of age. Today, we can reasonably expect to live to be at least seventy-six.

Today's midlifers are people who were born roughly between 1946 and 1965—the traditional baby boom generation. But whatever our chronological age, midlife is what happens to us when we finally grow up. It's a life transition that is every bit as confusing as adolescence, and just as challenging.

At midlife we are at the peak of our powers. We are responsible fathers and mothers; we are dutiful children to our parents; we are pillars of the community. In short, we are in the driver's seat. But just as we begin to wonder, *is that all there is?* the ground shifts. Physically our bodies start to show some wear and tear. We often feel as though we're going through an emotional roller-coaster ride. Our parents are aging and we become responsible for the lives of the very people who have always taken care of us. Our children are leaving, our jobs are changing, and retirement looms.

Midlife: A Manual is a friendly guide for those of us in midlife who find ourselves bewildered or even panic-striken by the turn our lives have taken. It's based on hands-on experience, and represents the collective wisdom of many people. With a little help from friends and experts, the authors have written about seven of the important issues we all face in our middle years. This book illuminates the journey we take through an often frustrating, sometimes enlightening, but never boring stage of life. We are in the middle of our lives, and there is more—much more—to come.

Midlife

A MANUAL

The Empty Nest

COLLEGE DAZE

When the time came for our daughter to go off to college, we were invited to a cocktail party for the parents of incoming freshmen who lived in the area. The hosts were transplants from Great Britain— very elegant, very rich and very intimidating to a couple of Brooklyn kids like us.

The guests ate, drank and became exceedingly merry because at long last the months of anxiety over college acceptances were finally over. Parents shared common experiences of life in the trenches—SAT cram courses, Ivy League rejections and interminable campus tours. We laughed at variations on the theme of The Great Interview Suit Disaster ("What do you *mean* it's at the dry cleaners? I have an interview in two hours. *Hello.*") and commiserated over nerve-shattering adolescent craziness through which we had managed to survive more or less intact.

Then someone mentioned the unmentionable: What about the empty nest? Our kids had driven us crazy. What would we do without them?

Sick as we were of dealing with seventeen-year-old angst, bored as we had become of listening to endless college tour litanies, and worried as most of us were about the cost of higher education, no one wanted to think about the emotional price we would have to pay when we said good-bye.

What had been chatty camaraderie a moment before became wistful silence. Then our elegant host spoke.

"Do you want to know the best thing about having our children away at college? Well, I'll tell you. Millie and I finally get to romp about the house naked—something we haven't been able to do since 1972."

One could only imagine what Frederick and Millicent looked like in the buff. Fred and Millie, age fifty-something, naked as jaybirds in the library, the morning room, the den. It boggled the mind. People smiled. Someone giggled. Perhaps we would survive the empty nest after all.

* * *

Your sentimental authors sometimes get nostalgic. We reminisce about the years gone by, when we jumped out of bed on wintry Saturday mornings to drive little Emma to her soccer games. Actually, it's quite charming to relive sweet memories while snuggling under the goose-down comforter on a snowy Saturday morning.

We have observed that it takes about a nanosecond for most parents to become accustomed to the reality of having their kids away at college. Once the shock wears off, the realization dawns:

You're free. You're no longer responsible for the daily care and feeding of an insatiable adolescent, and you don't have to worry about enforcing curfews. It's exhilarating.

> My daughter went off to college—and the dog died. For the first time in my life, I don't have to be a caretaker.
>
> —*Pattie, age forty-seven*

College is like summer camp, only it lasts longer. Ask any parent of a college student—they're home much more than they're on campus. Like the swallows to Capistrano, your young collegiate will return to the nest often, laden with sacks of dirty laundry and the phone numbers of friends in faraway places. Don't be surprised if your telephone bill begins to resemble the national debt.

College is a training ground for everyone. Children experience the pleasures of controlled independence, and their parents the forgotten joys of pre-offspring freedom. It's like being on a sabbatical.

POINT TO PONDER
The art of being wise is the art of knowing what to overlook.

—William James
The Principles of Psychology

WITH THE KIDS AWAY, YOU CAN:

1. Go on vacation when school is in session.

2. Make love in the morning.

3. Walk naked around the house.

4. Watch X-rated films with the doors open.

5. Play *your* kind of music.

6. Get into the bathroom.

7. Talk on the phone for a really long time.

8. Have time to read.

9. Find out what your partner has been thinking.

10. Eat out on Wednesday.

11. Be selfish without guilt.

12. Really appreciate your absent child. Bask in the knowledge that he or she is secretly beginning to appreciate you in a new way.

13.

14.

15.

(Use the last three spaces to fill in your own wish list.)

LETTING GO IS HARD TO DO

Some lucky families slide gracefully into post-college life. Children marry and create new nests or get jobs and establish their own centers of gravity. Mom and Dad renew their relationship and discover the joys of an extra bedroom. Everyone moves on.

Alas, life is often not so easy, and many families have a hard time making the transition. Paraphrasing Tolstoy, every struggling family struggles in its own way.

Here's what Michele says about letting go of her son:

❧ My older son is still struggling to find himself. He won't admit it, but he's economically dependent on us. He moved to California to get away, but we're still supporting him. He's nearly twenty-seven, but in some ways it feels like he's still in college. It's difficult to make the transition. We tend to give him unwanted advice. Giving advice and giving money are the two things we can do. It's a double-edged sword, because by being able to give him some money, we can also control him. If he didn't have to come to us for money, he probably wouldn't come to us for very much of anything, although when something's going wrong, we hear about it right away. When it's going right, it may take a while.

Recently, his girlfriend was in town on a business trip, and we went out to dinner. She casually mentioned how happy our son was at his job, what a nice apartment they had, and how well things seemed to be going for them. I realized this was something I would never hear from him. I only get gloom and doom.

It's easy to fall into the role of crisis manager. What used to be functional—the role of caregiver, parent, nurturer—can become dysfunctional when it prevents your child from taking responsibility for his/her life.

Here's the scenario: Your kid creates a crisis and you resolve it, usually with an infusion of money. Parents who find themselves caught up in this lose-lose situation don't believe they have any other role to play except that of banker. As Michele said, *If he didn't have to come to us for money, he probably wouldn't come to us for very much of anything.* Actually, your grown-up child needs your help moving on to the next rung of life's ladder—that of adult.

POINT TO PONDER
I suppose youth must be served,
but I'm sick and tired of serving it.

—Somerset Maugham
Of Human Bondage

It may well be that both you and your adult child are ambivalent. Your kid wants to become an independent adult, while at the same time he or she is yearning to be taken care of. And you're reluctant to give up the role of caregiver but at the same time you probably resent the responsibility of taking care of this able-bodied person. In Michele's case, money that might be used to support retirement is going to her son instead.

Ray told us he and his wife have forced themselves to leave the house on Sunday. They had gotten into the habit of waiting around for the *occasional* phone call from their daughter, who has moved to Italy. Every Sunday they were torn between their love for their daughter and their anger that she was "forcing" them to give up their Sunday pleasures.

Here's one mother's musings about the painful transition she was making with her grown children.

❧ It's like learning a new language. You have to learn to treat them in a different way. Sometimes I feel like I'm walking on eggshells, and I have to count to ten. What do I want? I'd like to be able to talk to my children as adult to adult, rather than parent to child. We try, but then we slip back into the old ways. My life is in limbo, because I haven't put closure on the life I have right now. Part of that is closure with parenting. I would feel more comfortable going ahead if I felt I wasn't needed in the same way as a parent.

—Pattie, age forty-seven

It's tough to shift gears. You've been responsible for so long, and now it's time to let go. It can be tricky. You want to help your child achieve independence, but at the same time, you don't want to send a message that you're no longer available.

How do you change the rules?

START A NEW RITUAL

Some family rituals are wonderful. They keep families from spinning off in a hundred different directions when things go bad. Other rituals just drag everyone down. They're things you do because you've been doing them for years, and no one really likes to do them, but, well, you've always done them, and what the heck.

POINT TO PONDER
One habit overcomes another.

—Thomas a Kempis
The Imitation of Christ

Think about a ritual you would love to eliminate from your life. Maybe you're sick of cooking Sunday dinner for everyone. When the children were young, it was an important weekly event that cemented the family unit. Now it's a drag, but you're afraid if you stop you'll never see them again. Could you replace this ritual with an activity that would make getting together more fun?

For example, instead of having everyone to your house for dinner every week, how about going out? Alternate who pays. If your child's finances don't allow for a fancy restaurant, why not suggest a coffee shop or diner? Or create the ritual of having your child pay the tip; you could also go Dutch treat.

This isn't about simply eating a meal. It's about changing perceptions of you as the Parental Figure (roll of drums, bugles sound) and your sons and daughters as eternal babies (infants wail) who are incapable of taking care of themselves. It's about creating an environment where you can get to know each other in a new way. It's about letting go of behavior that doesn't serve any purpose except to keep going through the same stale ritual.

REVERSING THE ROLES

Ask your child for advice and then really listen. You may find it a relief not to have to be all-knowing all the time, and besides, two heads really *are* better than one.

You can acknowledge to your kids that they have acquired life experiences that make their opinions valuable. You're validating their new role as adults. You're letting them know that they are capable of giving good advice and that you're capable of taking it. You're communicating that you're no longer the Omnipotent Parent.

LEARNING TO HAVE FUN

Go to a movie or a sporting event together. It doesn't matter what you do, as long as it creates a new pattern of sharing experiences.

✦ My daughter is in transition from college and looking for work. It is a tricky time in her life and it's hard getting along. She is thriving, she's very focused and very engaged. But I get the brunt of whatever she's going through. We can't really share much because she gets on my case about everything. I've discovered that movies are perfect. On some level she still needs me. In a dark movie house we can listen to someone else's troubles. Sometimes we talk about it afterwards, and sometimes we don't. I'm trying to understand. I know she is struggling to be her own person, to separate and come to terms with me, her father and herself. But sometimes I feel like a prison guard who's stuck with a hostile prisoner.

—*Esther, age forty-four*

WHEN TO EMPTY THE NEST

Shouldn't we want our offspring to come back home after college? Shouldn't we welcome them with open arms? Are we unfeeling and downright unnatural for wanting our independence from the parental role? Shouldn't we feel flattered that they want to stay with us instead of making a fast break for freedom?

Among the challenges of child rearing, helping our young achieve independence ranks up there with toilet training. We all know some things can't be learned secondhand. Stuff like how to hold down a nine-to-five job for more than three months, balance a checkbook, cook an egg, survive in a strange town. Think of it as basic training. There are lots of good reasons why you should help your son or daughter achieve independence. Sometimes, these reasons are urgent:

1. When you feel as though you're on opposite sides of a never-ending, intergenerational war.
2. When your offspring is too frightened to make the break and uses the homestead to hide out from life.
3. When you and your grown child have lifestyles that seriously conflict.
4. When you feel like an intruder in your own home.
5. When your son or daughter is a substance abuser and refuses treatment.
6. When privacy becomes a critical issue.

THE GREAT ABANDONMENT
(. . . And After All We've Done For You)

Children leaving the nest can cause an identity crisis for their parents. When you are no longer responsible for a child twenty-four hours a day, seven days a week, then who are you?

Don't be surprised if you feel blue and lonesome when your

child takes off for good. You may find yourself wandering into the vacant bedroom and sometimes even crying. Many parents have found themselves sleeping in their child's bed.

And, don't expect that you and your spouse will have the same reaction to your child's leaving home. Being a parent doesn't mean the same thing to everybody. Additionally, it's hard to be supportive when you're hurting. What can you do?

Allow yourself to have the feelings of abandonment. Even though you're still a parent, it's the end of a stage of life that can never be recaptured. You will get over it, but it may take some time.

> ✦ We didn't sleep together for two weeks after Michael left. My husband, Sam, slept in our son's bed. It made me crazy. It coincided with Sam having trouble at work. I wondered if there was a connection.
>
> —*Rachel, age fifty-nine*

> ✦ When my daughter left, I really became preoccupied with how long I needed to work before I could retire. It's funny how I began to allow myself to fantasize about not working and at the same time to get very anxious. If she was living with me, I bet I wouldn't even think about retiring, and getting old.
>
> —*Howie, age forty-seven*

When the nest is empty, you may be tempted to make a major change in your home. You may think of converting the kid's room into a studio, an office, or guest room. Our advice is to leave things alone for a year or two. At the very least, don't throw out, sell or redecorate anything that belongs to your children without asking their permission. It helps a grown child to be able to reenter the old world, still intact, while transitioning into a new life. Remember, despite the bravado, it is as difficult for the child as it is for you.

* * *

We live in a New York City apartment. Not a luxurious apartment by any means. Every square inch is valuable. Every nook and cranny contains something important. In fact, our daughter's bedroom is a converted dining alcove adjacent to the kitchen. It's a cute little hideaway that we would love to convert into an extended kitchen. Whenever we bring it up, Emma throws a fit. It can't be done yet. In the meantime, we are quietly collecting pictures of our dream kitchen. Tune in next year . . .

BOOMERANG KIDS

POINT TO PONDER

Bliss it was that dawn to be alive,
But to be young was very heaven!

—William Wordsworth
The French Revolution

We fondly remember our post-college days: bricks and boards, Indian-print bedspreads on the windows, scrambled tofu with brown rice for breakfast. We moved out of our parents' home, loudly proclaimed our independence, and slipped into an environment where we didn't have to go it alone. In retrospect, the communes and group living that we chose were essentially halfway houses. Divided among several people the rent was cheap (and the food dreadful), but the place was ours. And it was fun.

Life is more complicated today. Panhandling isn't cool, and street people aren't romantic—they're homeless and in desperate need of help. Apartments are expensive—just about anything with four walls and a ceiling is being sold at a premium. Communal living is passé, and all the great old apartments where we used to crash in the good old days have been turned into luxury dwellings or reconfigured into studios.

Why do kids return to the nest? They come back to save money, to attend school, or because they're having financial difficulties. Sometimes they simply can't afford the rents, to say nothing of buying a condo or co-op. They may also come back because they're not psychologically prepared to live apart from us. Sociologists call these returners "boomerang kids."

Kids who come to live at home after moving out have had a taste of freedom. They are different from offspring who haven't yet made the transition to independence because they know what it's like to live away from parental authority. They've incompletely transitioned into adulthood.

Meanwhile, the parents of these kids have gotten used to living without them. When children become independent, parents often have more discretionary income and a level of personal freedom that is harder to achieve when they have dependent youngsters in their care.

Boomerang kids can create problems. Parents often need to halt their own life transitions so they can support their grown children, both financially and emotionally.

Old patterns can be hard to change. An offspring may be a fully grown adult. But when your kid comes back to the nest, it's easy to fall into the old parent-child relationship, as inappropriate as that relationship may have become. It takes work to change the rules and adopt a living arrangement that takes into account each of your adult needs.

Some families find they are able to accommodate each other in ways that are mutually beneficial. These parents feel that having their children's friendship and day-to-day companionship more than compensates for the financial and social inconvenience boomerang kids often represent. Their children find living in their parents' home helps them make important transitions into adulthood, such as reaching a professional goal, returning to school, or saving money for marriage. It does not automatically mean the kid doesn't want to grow up. It may be a sign of a close-knit relationship. After all, an offspring who can't tolerate his/her parents isn't likely to come back unless there's a dire emergency.

Ironically, we may be making it easier for our kids to return to the nest. Sociologists report what we've suspected: There's less of a generation gap between parents and grown children today than the one which existed between us and our parents.

> ✢ My older son came back home for about a year and a half while he was trying to get his career going. He was working for himself, so not paying rent made a big difference.
>
> Having my son come back to live with me was a mixed bag. It was mostly wonderful. The major issue was that I was a single woman, and it did interfere with dating, because I wouldn't bring men back to the house. It was just too awkward. The problem was, it became too easy in some

ways not to date because my son was a wonderful companion. He and I both talked about it, and we agreed finally that he really had to move out of the house, in part just for that reason. It was a little too perfect for both of us.

He began dating, but there was never a conflict with him having a girlfriend and living at home. That's never been an issue. We treated the situation as if we were roommates—housemates—because we both felt it was the only way the setup would work. For example, I did not come home to cook for him. If one of us cooked, we made enough for the other.

And I don't mean this was easy, and I don't mean I didn't always come home, especially if I was worried about him. What I mean to say is that we made an effort to treat each other like adults. We shared responsibilities and restrictions. We were both free to come and go as we pleased with the only restriction on both of us being, "Just let me know where you're going or if you're going to be out all night," so we wouldn't worry or call the police.

—*Natalie, age forty-eight*

Many young adults who choose to live at home with their parents say the experience has led to a more mature relationship between them. At its best, having a child at home can add a youthful spirit to the house. Should you agree to let your child move back home? Well, that depends.

The following self evaluation test can help you decide if your kid will prosper from staying at home and whether you'll enjoy such a relationship.

SELF EVALUATION SHEET

These questions require some soul-searching. Be honest. If you come to the conclusion that you really can live with your offspring, ask him/her to fill out the same questionnaire. Don't show the answers to each other. This isn't an encounter group. It's simply meant to help you individually figure out if living together is the right choice for you.

1) What will the financial arrangements be?

    a) Will your child be living rent free?

    b) Will he/she help with any extraneous expenses?

    c) Will you be expected to help him/her financially? (Is the child employed?)

2) What kind of relationship do you have with your child?

    a) Has there been much contact between you recently?

    b) Do you generally get along?

    c) Are you comfortable with the way you handle disagreements?

3) Can your home comfortably accommodate your child's return?

    a) Does your home have enough space to provide privacy for each of you?

    b) Do you have ground rules in place for such "hot button" issues as sex, alcohol, drugs, overnight guests, parties?

4) Can you see your child as an independent adult? Do you still view him/her as your baby?

5) Does your child treat you like an adversary?

6) Imagine that you were interviewing for a roommate and your child came to the interview. How would you react?

7) Can you talk to him/her about your concerns?

8) List three things that you absolutely can't stand about your child's behavior. Be honest. Now ask yourself if you can live with these traits.

WHEN YOU CAN'T EMPTY THE NEST

Some people can't empty the nest because their kids are developmentally or emotionally unable to cope with independence.

❧ We have two grown sons. One is a lawyer with a wife and child. Our other son is a paranoid schizophrenic. He used to have his own apartment, and he only stayed with us over the weekends. But, little by little he turned the two-day weekend into a four-day weekend, and now he lives here all the time. It's very comfortable for him and very difficult for us. He doesn't like to be alone, and on the other hand, he doesn't like to share an apartment with another person.

We would love to have an empty nest. We're tired. We're tired of taking care of somebody else. We're ready to take care of ourselves without having him in the equation. It changes the way we live. We're tied to the house more than we'd like to be. We have to prepare food. There's an extra burden—a child who has never grown up. Now we're coming to the conclusion that unless something very special happens—the discovery of a medication that he responds to—that this will be our life for many, many years to come. And that really makes the situation even more difficult. We're getting older. We'd like to travel—we've always wanted to travel, and we can't.

—*Madeleine, age fifty-eight; Stuart, age sixty-two*

If your child is emotionally disabled, don't expect to tackle it on your own. Families in this difficult situation need to get in touch with organizations that have support groups for parents. Significantly, many of these organizations also function as advocates for the severely mentally ill. They lobby for public- and private-sector funding in support of new treatment technologies. (See the Resources at the end of this chapter.)

With the support of these agencies, parents of emotionally challenged children also need to make their voices heard on some very crucial issues. These include:

- The development of housing alternatives that provide your child with a safe environment and one that offers opportunities to acquire social, educational, and vocational skills.
- Elimination of the stigma that is associated with mental illness.
- Dissemination of information about new and more effective medications and other treatment technologies, such as assertive community treatment.
- Commitment to the concept of rehabilitation and recovery as an integral part of treatment.
- Commitment to an ongoing dialogue between family members and people receiving mental health services.

⟶ My daughter is developmentally disabled, and she also has emotional problems. She was on a very long waiting list for supportive housing, but she finally was contacted.

It's been a very important life change for her, and for us. She's discovering that she's able to do things she was never confident enough to try.

As for us, for the first time in years, we've been able to

have a reasonable life. Our sex life used to be just a memory, but we're getting the hang of it again. It's great.

—Wanda, age fifty-two

POINT TO PONDER

Kids don't often turn out to be the sorts of people their parents want them to be, or they often do not do the sorts of things their parents imagined or wished for them. Part of saying good-bye is hoping that your children will become what they want to be. Success as a parent is not determined by whether or not your kids become doctors or investment bankers. Rather, it is shown in your children's feeling free to become the individuals they want to be and feeling clear that their lives are their own.

—Alan Siegel, Ed.D.
Associate Professor, Harvard Medical School

We spend years raising our children. We worry about their future. We obsess about their health, their schooling, their love lives (or lack thereof). Our hearts and minds are totally absorbed in the loving tasks of parenting. We put our own dreams on hold; maybe we forgot we ever had them. This work sheet is designed to help you remember. Its purpose is to get you to start thinking and talking about it.

SELF EVALUATION TEST:
THIS IS YOUR LIFE

1. When the kids were in the house, I dreamed of doing the following but couldn't:

2. Now I'm free to follow my dream of:

3. Now my significant other and I can begin to realize our dream of:

4. I (we) have really outgrown:

The Empty Nest: Recommended Reading

And Suddenly They're Gone: What Parents Need to Know About the Empty Nest, by Patricia S. Olson, Tiffany Press, 1993

Empty Nest. . . Full Heart: The Journey from Home to College, by Andrea Van Steenhouse, Johanna Parker, Simpler Life Press, 1998.

How to Survive and Thrive in an Empty Nest: Reclaiming Your Life When Your Children Have Gone, by Jeanette C. Lauer, Robert H. Lauer, New Harbinger Publications, 1999.

Resources—USA

For parents of mentally ill adult children: NAMI-FACT (National Association for the Mentally Ill-Families and Consumers Together)

632 Broadway
Suite 32
New York, NY 10012
212-677-8054

The New World of Work

We are in the middle of a revolution in the workplace. Assumptions about loyalty and long-term commitment are giving way to rapid-fire decisions based on quarterly reports and the seismic shifts of a global market.

The safety net is gone, and we are perplexed and a little frightened by it all.

Living in "interesting times" can be a curse or a blessing. Oftentimes, it's both. Interesting times can mean dislocation—physical, social, emotional. They're times of test and challenge, of suffering and insecurity. Bedrock becomes sand under your feet. You will be tested. You will be asked to do more than you want to do, and you will be required to rise to the challenge or fall behind.

➴ I think what has changed in the workplace is the rate of change. In the past, a worker could have gone twenty years before noticing that his workplace had changed to such a degree that he no longer recognized it. All of a sudden, in the last two or three years, the rate of change has become vastly accelerated, and the kinds of changes have been very, very dramatic.

—Ed, psychiatrist, age forty-two

You are in the middle of your life, and you never asked for this turmoil. That is the curse.

Here's the blessing: You will discover new dimensions to yourself. You will be given yet another chance to recreate your life, given all the knowledge you've gained over the past years.

Here's another blessing. We can expect to live longer and healthier lives than anyone in the history of the human race, and in all likelihood, we can expect to work longer too. After all, if we are healthy and enjoy what we do, it's absurd to quit simply because social convention dictates it's time to stop.

Experts predict that in the twenty-first century, less than half the U.S. workforce will be in conventional, full-time jobs. Already, jobs ranging from CEO to janitor are being converted into non-permanent positions. Independent contractors and temporary staff are replacing full-time workers.

It's time to consider nontraditional options. In the past, some of us may have viewed temporary, part-time and volunteer work as unacceptable, except in emergencies. Today, many of us will find ourselves giving serious consideration to part-time, freelance, temporary, consulting, subcontracting or seasonal work as well as job sharing.

If you've been laid off from a large corporation, keep in mind that companies with fewer than one thousand employees tend to value older, more experienced workers. More than 90 percent of all firms in the United States employ fewer than five hundred people, and for the last several years, they have been responsible for 75 percent of all new hires. Consider targeting smaller companies when you plan your job-hunting strategy.

POINT TO PONDER

It is weariness to keep toiling at the same things so that one becomes ruled by them.

—Heraclitus

Let's face it. Some of us knew what we wanted to do with the rest of our lives when we were five, but most of us floundered around until we found a niche that more or less fit. Many people have a dream that was deferred or a vocation that was discovered at the worst possible time in life.

If you've been thinking of changing professions and find yourself unemployed, view this hiatus as a chance to reevaluate what you've done professionally and to explore new options. It's a time to reassess what's important to you now, in contrast to what you valued when you first entered the workforce.

Now is the time to take stock of what you'd like to do. Being between jobs offers you an extraordinary opportunity to reinvent yourself, rethink who you want to be, and begin a new journey.

❧ When I was forty-four, I was laid off from my job as administrative assistant to the director of communications in a large pharmaceutical company. I had always wanted to go into publishing, but when I was a kid, I couldn't afford it. Publishing is notorious for paying rock-bottom salaries at the entry level. It was kind of catch-22—now that I was married and could afford to start at the bottom, I was too old. I mean, nobody was interested in a forty-four-year-old apprentice editor.

I decided I had nothing to lose, so I applied at an employment agency, and there was an entry-level job available—an editorial assistant. I was ten years older than my boss and fifteen years older than my co-workers. The reason my boss hired me was because I wasn't afraid of computers, and he was terrified. The East Coast had just discovered them, and most people didn't even know how to turn one on. I didn't know much, but in that place I was a genius. I absolutely loved working in publishing. I paid my dues, worked fourteen-hour days—weekends too—and eventually worked my way up to senior editor.

You have to think positive and not get into the mindset of being old. Of course, if you go into something new, you also have to accept that you may be making less money. That's part of the deal.

—*Sally, editor, age fifty-four*

PROFESSIONAL NETWORKING

If you have the feeling that you're becoming vulnerable because of downsizing or a trend toward hiring less expensive, albeit less experienced workers, it's time to network.

First, go through your Rolodex or electronic organizer and identify people from other companies whom you've worked well with and with whom you've had good experiences. Each day, make it a point to call at least four of your contacts. Let them know you're exploring new opportunities and that you're open to new ventures. See where the conversation takes you. They may keep you in mind, mentally "bookmarking" you and your assets for future employment or even a current opening. Or they may suggest someone else or a firm with whom they have a connection or working relationship. Their positive referral may result in a new job.

POINT TO PONDER
Your phone list is a very powerful job-hunting tool.

Another powerful way to network professionally is to use your current job to "audition" for a position with another firm. Your current responsibilities may involve collaborating with staff of another organization on a specific project. Use this opportunity to showcase your talents. You never know when a job will become available, or when a staff member with whom you've worked will be asked if he/she knows anyone who might be interested in a position.

USING THE INTERNET IN
YOUR JOB SEARCH

It's not a magic bullet, but if you're looking for a job, it's worth your while to check out the Internet. Sites list jobs, recruiters and placement firms. You can also find lists or publications and directories of people. But, remember, simply being listed in a directory is not necessarily an endorsement. Some people are listed because they've paid a fee to have their names included. Check out their track record and how long they've been out there.

Several books are available that can teach you how to access online bulletin boards, job listings, recruiters, discussion groups and resume posting services. (See Resources.) Once you get your feet wet, you'll be able to scout for opportunities online and send applications and resumes through e-mail.

While the Internet can't replace networking and other traditional ways of finding work, it's become an important resource in our modern world.

The Web sites we've listed are just a few of the many job banks available online (See Resources).

VOLUNTEER AND PART-TIME WORK:
WHY VOLUNTEER?

Volunteer work used to be a stepchild. People gave lip service to "do-gooders," but privately many thought it was a step down to work for free. It's time to rethink that perception. If you're looking to change professions, volunteering may be your best bet.

> ❧ I worked with an aged population, but after twenty years, I was burnt out and needed a change. For a long time I thought about shifting gears and counseling young people, but I didn't have the specific skills, and I couldn't afford to quit work and go back to school.

I volunteered to work with troubled kids in a house of detention. It's been a trade-off. I have strong administrative skills, and they have the clients I want to learn how to work with. It's not easy—I have to give up some personal time, and I'm tired a lot. The work is very demanding, but I'm finding it well worth the effort.

—*Lloyd, social worker, age forty-two*

Volunteering in a new field can help you decide if you want to pursue it further. You also can gain experience or sharpen your skills in a field you already know. Being a volunteer is an excellent way to test the waters and make new contacts. And you can put the experience you gain as a volunteer on your resumé.

Experts advise job-seekers who have done volunteer work to include the experience on their resumés. You're not required to indicate that it was unpaid work. In other words, describe what you did, the activities or people you may have supervised, and the skills you've acquired, as well as training or classes in which you participated.

Volunteering is also an opportunity to help others. It's a way to stay active when you're unemployed and to keep some perspective on your own situation.

HOW TO VOLUNTEER

- Choose an organization you like or one in which you have some personal interest.
- Check your local newspaper and public agencies for volunteer opportunities.

- The Red Cross and United Way have thousands of volunteer opportunities in many areas, including administration, human relations and management.
- The Internet lists thousands of volunteer opportunities. Use a keyword search.
- If you're computer literate, think about volunteering your time off-site. CompuMentor (www.compumentor.org) offers volunteer-based computer assistance to schools and nonprofit organizations.

POINT TO PONDER

It has been computed by some political arithmetician that if every man and woman would work for four hours each day on something useful, that labor would produce sufficient to procure all the necessaries and comforts of life. Want and misery would be banished out of the world and the rest of the twenty-four hours might be leisure and pleasure.

—Benjamin Franklin

If you love the work you do but have been downsized, think about working part time, working from your home or becoming a consultant.

CONSULTING

A friend, Carla, who is in her forties, is a vice president at a large medical center. She changed careers several times before finding her niche. We asked her what she might do if she were laid off tomorrow:

> ✦ I would try to assess what it was I wanted to do, what my skills are, and my interests. I think at this point, if it happened to me tomorrow, maybe I would go out on my own. I've always thought about starting my own business and it would give me the motivation, the kick, the push to finally do something that I always wanted to do but couldn't.
>
> The financial issues are a big concern . . . would I have enough money to pay my bills? Maybe I would look for another position while I was doing it, maybe I'd work part time somewhere while I was trying to build something up on the side.
>
> I think it's a great time to take stock and to re-group, and I wouldn't be as panicked as I would have been at twenty-five or thirty-five if I was laid off. Although it's more important for me to have a steady income now, I'm more in control. When I was younger, I remember I panicked when I was laid off. I had to get another job immediately. I didn't even take the time to understand what it was I wanted to do. So I think it's a wonderful opportunity to assess what you want to do with the rest of your life.

Another friend recently quit a prestigious job in a major

publishing house to become an independent consultant. Here's what he said:

> ❧ I worked in publishing for twenty years, and if it had not been for my companion, Ed, convincing me that sometimes a new move makes a great deal of sense, I probably would not have had the courage to quit. But I wasn't happy in corporate publishing. There was too much business and too little editing. I wanted to focus on editorial work, which was the reason I went into publishing in the first place—the love of books and the chance to work with an author on the manuscript.
>
> The minute I left my job, everything seemed to fall into place. I got a number of terrific clients to work with and business is going very well. I really love the flexibility I have working out of my own apartment.
>
> As recently as a year and a half ago, when people told me they were doing something like independent consulting, I would shiver at the very idea that they didn't know where their next paycheck was coming from.
>
> I grew up with a very strict sense that you had to belong to a very paternalistic company so you'd know exactly when you'd be paid and exactly what kind of work you would be doing. Everything had to be very set. In fact, it *is* very set in a big company, but it can also be suffocating.
>
> I'm probably one of the most risk-adverse people in the world, but Ed helped me see that you can use the risk as fuel to help you to do the things you've always wanted to

do. I guess I had to wrap my mind around that thought and make it a reality instead of running from it.

—Jay, editor, age forty-two

THE NEW TECHNOLOGY

Whether you're working at a job that has recently begun to rely on computers or looking for new employment, computers are the key to your professional survival, to say nothing of success in today's job market. If you can't use a computer, you are at an enormous disadvantage.

✤ It's obvious that the thrust in my particular situation is technology, and when this first started happening [computers], I made no bones about how I felt. I think some of it is ridiculous. For example, I don't think you can be a good counselor to a young girl with an eating disorder by plugging in the computer and finding an article about anorexia, although it is helpful. I think technology is a good tool. I don't think it's a "be-all" or "end-all." I think a lot of it is bullshit. To be a better counselor, I should really focus on the kids. I do try to keep up with things . . . I certainly have become much more proficient using a computer than I was. I'm still in the beginning stages but certainly more than I ever thought I could be.

—Michele, guidance counselor, age fifty-four

We've been there. Last year, Steve turned on our brand-new Gateway 2000 and saw the Windows screen for the first time. He hit the roof. He was sure the company had made a mistake. They had accidentally sent us a computer programmed for a five-year-old, with music designed to tranquilize a fractious child, a little trash bin logo and an animated paper clip that winked and minced in the corner of the monitor ("It looks like you're writing a letter. Want help?"). Furious, he unplugged the machine (resulting in a minor Windows catastrophe, but that's another story) and wept for his prehistoric Wordstar software. True, the Wordstar program required that he learn more codes than a CIA operative, but at least it had dignity. Steve wept for his self-correcting Selectric with the whirling ball, the Royal electric it replaced and the Smith Corona manual he had bought for eighty-five dollars in 1960.

We understand. We sympathize. Nonetheless, we strongly recommend that you don't confide to your co-workers that your idea of ideal office equipment is an abacus and quill. Instead, we suggest you communicate your excitement at staying on the cutting edge. Let your boss and co-workers know how interested you are in the prospect of learning new programs and linking your extensive knowledge of the job with the new computer-based technology. (If you must throw up, do it later and in private.)

How do you become computer savvy without going nuts? First of all, take advantage of training programs your employer may offer and learn everything you can. Remember, knowledge is power, and a free class that teaches the new technology is a trade-off for dwindling job security. Think of it as money in the bank. It's also good public relations to be seen as an employee who's actively working to get up to speed.

If you're looking for a job, don't fool yourself into thinking you don't need to upgrade your skills. Beg, borrow or buy a state-of-the-art computer. If you happen to own a vintage model, we suggest you keep it. (We threw out our "antique" 1984 computer when we moved. It was the first portable ever produced, and today it's a collector's item.)

Don't panic if you haven't a clue how to turn on a computer. It's time to strategize. This is war. Enroll in a class for computer illiterates at your local community college. Don't be afraid. The kids who teach these classes have parents who were every bit as uncomfortable as you are now. These kids speak technophobe, and they're very nice people. Or let your own children teach you what they know about the basics. (It's a good way to bond.) You can also put an ad in the local college newspaper and hire a student to give you lessons. Finally, don't forget that every computer program has a tutorial built into the system. It's free. Use it.

❧ When I moved to the city from the suburbs, I found that the business world had changed. I used to work part time in an insurance office. We didn't have computers. I had an electric typewriter, but we were very old fashioned. I should have left that job and learned computers, but you can't see the future.

This past year my sons pushed me into it. They bought me a computer with Windows 95 and set it up in the living room, and they started giving me lessons. And then I sat down and began to play with it. I'd call one of my sons in a panic and tell him, "I can't get out of this screen" and he'd help me. I'm now on the Internet and I e-mail friends in Philadelphia and California. I can type a letter and print it out. The boys really pulled me into the year 2000, kicking and screaming.

—Rachel, secretary, age fifty-nine

Personally, we've never found computer books to be particularly helpful, but some folks swear by them. You may want to check out what's available at your local library or bookstore.

AGE DISCRIMINATION

❧ When I was thirty-six and working in the marketing department of a publisher of educational material, my company was sold. Rumors began to circulate that they were replacing the president, who was a fifty-one-year-old woman, with a twenty-eight-year-old man. I was already seeing younger people coming into the company.

At the time, though, I also thought it would be interesting to become involved with health-care marketing, and so the impetus to move on wasn't created by a fear of age discrimination, but it certainly was strengthened by what was going on.

Two months after I left, they fired the woman and put the kid in her place. Someone in payroll leaked that he was making thirty grand less.

—*Etta, marketing, age forty-four*

❧ I was interviewed by a young woman in her late twenties. She calls me in, and I'm sitting there telling her about the job I used to have, and she says, "Well, you know you have to answer a *lot* of phone calls here, this is a *newspaper*." And I say, "Yes, I know. I worked in an insurance company for thirteen years. I answered a lot of phones." And she says, "Well, it's very, very, very busy here." We talk and talk, but when I leave the office I think, "That arrogant snotnose! Talking to me like I'm senile!"

—*Maureen, secretary, age fifty-eight*

Age discrimination is poisonous for many reasons. The first, obviously, is that well-trained and qualified workers are put out of work. The second, more insidious reason is that it creates a destructive sense of hopelessness in the person who's on the receiving end.

Don't drink the poison. Whether you've been laid off because of downsizing, let go because a younger person is coming in for less money, passed over for a position because of your age, or laid off because your job has been deemed obsolete, you are essentially the same person you were last year. Now is the time to repair your self-image.

We believe the most constructive way to deal with age discrimination is to use the anger and frustration to fuel your ambition. Get even by using this time in your life to discover new skills and develop new outlets for your talents.

> ❧ I was laid off around my fifty-fifth birthday. I'd been working for the same company all those years—there'd been rumblings about downsizing, but who thinks it's gonna happen to you? The bastards hired a kid out of school—I mean, a kid younger than my sons. It killed me. I'm embarrassed to say it now, but I sat in the house and cried like a baby.
>
> Well, eventually—I'd say a couple of months—my wife read me the riot act. I went to a counselor, who told me that I was in mourning. Maybe she was right.
>
> So finally, I started pulling myself together. I made some phone calls. It was hard. I was hired to do some small consulting jobs. Then a guy I used to work with called. He was teaching a math class in a community college, and they needed someone who could go in on Saturday mornings.
>
> Today, I do consulting out of my home. I work one day a week for a small company, and I teach at the community college. I like teaching and I'm thinking of starting a tutoring service with a couple of buddies. You know,

math, physics, computer technology. The kids have an expression, "Get a life." Well, I got one.

—*Jerome, electrical engineer, age fifty-eight*

WHEN YOUR BOSS IS (MUCH) YOUNGER THAN YOU

POINT TO PONDER

All clues, no solutions. That's the way things are.

—Dennis Potter
The Singing Detective

❧ The new Vice Principal could be my son. Sometimes he still refers to me as "Mrs. _____" and I refer to him as "Fred." He plays New Age music in the office.

The other day, this "English as a Second Language" teacher had three kids asking the staff, "Do you remember where you were when Kennedy died?" There are people on staff who weren't even *born* when Kennedy died. Afterwards, I asked the teacher, "How did they know who to go to?" and she said, "Well, don't take this wrong but the kids went around saying, 'Oh, she's old—we'll ask her.'" They knew exactly who to talk to. They looked at certain members of staff, and they said, "We'll ask this one—she's old."

—*Michele, guidance counselor, age fifty-four*

We've heard lots of anecdotes about what it's like to work with a boss or group of people who are much younger. ("*No, Jimmy Hendrix was not one of the Beatles.*") It's tempting to use their age as an opportunity to rail against everything else that's changing in the workplace. But you know, your boss or co-workers have jobs they've been hired to do. They are probably intimidated by your years of experience, and if they are arrogant, they may well be covering their fear. You may have kids their age, but you probably remind them of their parents. You may be younger than springtime in your ability to think creatively on the job, but to a twenty-seven-year-old, you're a parental figure. That's life, so cut the kid some slack.

We asked an older guy who works in the civil service how he negotiates the age hurdles. Here's his irreverent response:

> ✤ Younger workers usually ask advice on intramural political problems. Middle-management supervisors concerned about power don't ask. Senior supervisors will sometimes ask about getting resources or technical problems, such as dealing with surveys, etc. I tell them what I know. I am respectful of my boss and colleagues. I complete my work. My hearing and memory preclude gossip.
>
> —*Maurice, accountant, age sixty-three*

POINT TO PONDER
Looking for a job is a very stressful job.

Job hunting is a job. Remember the "good old days," when you were employed at a nine-to-five job? Did you bound out of bed every single, solitary morning with a song in your heart? Was every day filled with unmitigated joy? If you answered yes to all of these questions, you're probably a saint and don't need to read this section.

For most of us, work is a mixed bag of good and bad experiences, of highs and lows. Now your job is looking for work. You're not always going to feel like beating the bushes, making the phone calls, networking, putting on your suit, and going out there. It's hard and plenty scary. Do it anyway. You've made it this far in life. Think of everything you've achieved. Now, take your experience and present it to the world as the asset it is rather than the liability you perceive it to be.

When you're out of work, it's important to keep your life in perspective. Being unemployed isn't business as usual; it's an extraordinarily stressful time. Your confidence is at a low ebb, and you may even be secretly thinking you're going to be unemployed forever. It's not so. Remember, you've been employed for much longer than you've been out of work. Think about your past accomplishments and what you're looking to achieve in the future. Take the long view.

While you're looking to the past for perspective and to the future for focus, don't forget to take care of yourself in the present. Eat properly, get plenty of sleep, and get people to help you—emotionally and spiritually. Your ego is fragile right now, and you may be feeling vulnerable.

We suggest that you surround yourself with people who love you and can be supportive. Don't expect one or two close friends or family members to do it all. Your need is great, and burnout even among those nearest and dearest to you can be high. Allow all your friends and loved ones to help get you through this difficult period. When they're in a similar spot, you'll be there for them.

Consider joining a support group for job hunters. It's helpful to be among people who all speak the same language. You'll be able to offer each other support and helpful advice. One group we particularly like is the Five O'Clock Club. (See Resources.) Also check out the *Wall Street Journal*'s "National Business and Employment Weekly" for other job clubs.

SURVIVAL TIPS

We all agree that looking for work is not the happiest of times. It's important to take care of yourself and give yourself perks.

- Spring for a ten-dollar manicure and a new hairdo or a haircut.
- Go to inexpensive plays and concerts with friends.
- If you've been very productive in pursuing leads, give yourself a special treat—go to the movies in the middle of the day. But don't fall into the trap of making it a habit. Take heed: Movies can be very seductive escapes from reality.
- Pretend you're a tourist in a new city. You're on the street during the day, a time when tourists are about. Practice viewing your familiar surroundings through fresh eyes.
- If you can afford it, buy yourself a new interview suit. Or spring for a new pair of shoes, a tie or a handbag to wear with a suit you already own.
- Get exercise and eat right. Remember, finding a new job is

not your punishment. You don't have to cloister yourself away in shame. You don't have to deny yourself pleasure.

- If you are a workaholic, this is a good time to give yourself a breather and take stock of what you want to do with the next period of your life.
- Use the time to your advantage, but remember, your job is finding a job.

You may find it helpful to talk to a spiritual advisor or to join a meditation group to help you gain perspective.

POINT TO PONDER

All will be well,

And all will be well

And every manner of thing

Will be well.

—Julian of Norwich
Book of Showings

The self examination test that follows is designed to help you take a closer look at your professional profile. It asks you to consider your strengths, your job potential and preferences, and the options you may have.

SELF EXAMINATION TEST: TAKING STOCK

1. What skills do I possess?

2. What did I like about my former job(s)?

3. What did I dislike?

4. Do I want to go back to school? □ Yes □ No

5. If yes, in what course of study am I interested?

6. Do I want to relocate? □ Yes □ No

7. If yes, what region(s) do I want to consider?

8. Do I want to change my lifestyle? □ Yes □ No

9. If yes, how?

10. What interests do I have that could be translated into paid employment?

11. Can volunteer or pro bono work I've done be translated into a new career? □ Yes □ No

12. If you answered yes, go into detail?

13. Can I afford to work at a lower salary? □ Yes □ No

14. If yes, how will I do it?

15. What is my dream career? Why?

16. Have I abandoned a career that I would like to explore? □ Yes □ No

17. If yes, what is it?

18. What job or field did I give up for a more lucrative career?

19. Is it too late for me to consider it now? □ Yes □ No

20. If you answered yes, why is that?

21. What training, further education or credentials would I need if I were to embark on my dream career?

22. What do I want my professional life to be like five years from now?

SELF EXAMINATION TEST:
WHEN YOU'RE UNEMPLOYED

I'm unemployed because:

The assets I bring to the job market are:

My past accomplishments include:

My goals for the next five years are:

Recommended Reading

101 Best Job Search Sites on the Internet, by Katherine K. Yonge, Linx Educational Publishers, 1998

The Guide to Internet Job Searching, by Margaret Riley, VGM Career Horizons, 1996

Losing Your Job—Reclaiming Your Soul, by Mary Lynn Pulley, Terrence E. Deal, Jossey-Bass Publishers, 1997

Resumes in Cyberspace: Your Complete Guide to a Computerized Job Search, by Pat Criscito, Barrons Educational Series, 1997

Workshift: How to Prosper in a Workplace Without Jobs, by William Bridges, Perseus Press, 1995

Resources

The Five O'Clock Club
300 East 40th Street
New York, NY 10016
www.5occ.com
800-538-6645 ext. 600

World Wide Web Job Banks

www.ajb.dni.us
America's Job Bank

www.careermosaic.com
Career Mosaic

www.careerpath.com
Career Path

www.espan.com
E-Span

www.monster.com
Monster Board

www.occ.com
Online Career Center

THREE

Exercise: The Treadmill of Life

POINT TO PONDER

Whenever I feel an urge to exercise, I lie down

until it goes away.

—Anonymous

Every age has its physical indignities. As infants we endured diaper rash, teething and immunization shots. Ouch! Later, came acne, nocturnal emissions, sanitary belts, wisdom teeth, braces, razor burn.

As we mature we are introduced to such medical delights as the mammogram, flexible sigmoidoscopy, pelvic sonogram, and prostate examination. All necessary. All good. All right—we do them but we don't have to smile.

At middle age, the chickens come home to roost. They roost in gut and backside, in blood pressure, cholesterol, bone density and prostate. Wherever. We find ourselves in an adversarial relationship with our bodies, and all the denial in the world can't hide the fact that if we don't take stock and do something to remedy the situation now, there'll be more hell to pay down the road.

So we try. We buy books that teach us how to go on healthy diets. We tell ourselves that healthful food is good medicine. Then we cheat, feel guilty, and buy some more books. We wonder whatever happened to the good old days, when the worst thing that could happen if we ate french fries and chocolate cake was an embarrassing eruption of pimples.

If we're disciplined, we reach a balance—a little junk food and a lot of low-fat nutrition. If we're not so disciplined, we may end up on medications to control our blood pressure, cholesterol level or bone density.

Unfortunately, there is no magic pill that allows us to eat like fifteen-year-olds and not suffer the consequences. But there are ways we can stay healthy without starving ourselves. One way is to search until we find a well-balanced diet that we can tolerate for more than a week. Another way is to exercise.

You've heard this a million times before, but listen again—it's important. Exercise reduces the risks of coronary artery disease, stroke, diabetes, high cholesterol and osteoporosis. It helps some people control depression, and it's a great way to burn calories.

We report this with some sadness because at least one of us would rather have her toenails pulled out at the root than engage in vigorous sport.

CONFESSIONS OF A COUCH POTATO
by Judith Estrine

Exercise is nature's way of tormenting me. It is boring, time consuming, occasionally painful, intermittently humiliating—did I forget to mention boring?

I was the kid who was hit in the head with the volleyball, got lost on the way to third base, and nearly drowned in the shallow end of the pool. My friends at the Freddie Fitzsimmons Bowling Alley couldn't believe my perfect score—not just anyone can bowl zero.

When I was grew up, I made the fatal mistake of falling in love with a long-distance runner. Worse, I married him. Steve was cagey. One Sunday morning just after we were married, he said, "I've got something important to say."

There he was, doing an absurd stretching exercise, looking ridiculously fit in his stupid little runner's shorts, while I lay curled on the sofa, the picture of Sunday contentment. "Great," I purred. "We'll talk when you get back."

"It can't wait."

"Then talk to me, lover. I'm all ears."

"No—run with me to the park. We'll talk there."

"The park?"

"Yeah—run with me to the park. What I have to say, I have to say in the park."

Until that moment, life had been sweet. Just me, my sofa, my coffee, my man. But now the snake was in the garden, and I was curious. Had my husband embezzled money? Lost his job? Fathered a love child?

. . . *So the newlywed fool ran, struggling to keep up with her husband, clutching her side as a stitch of pain ripped into her tender vitals. . ..*

I waited tactfully for the dark secret to be revealed. What in the world could it be? Finally, as I prepared to die, Steve murmured, "I absolutely adore you. Do you understand? You're here so I can tell you I want to share my world of running with you."

Not true. I was there because I was a jerk. So I decked him, right? Well, not exactly. It's true the guy manipulated me. Played me like a violin. However, in my heart of hearts, I believe that terms of endearment between a married couple are as precious as diamonds. I couldn't very well spit in his eye, could I?

I finished the run, sweating like a pig and silently praying that the Angel of Death would have mercy and either smite me or my beloved. Preferably my beloved.

The second time Steve conned me, I was marginally less traumatized because now I knew the landmarks. The big rock was about a minute away from the water fountain, and if I made it that far, I could legitimately stop for a drink. After that, I was halfway home. How did he get me out this time? Bribery. The guy was shameless. He bought me a sweet little purple running outfit that made me feel like an athlete—a clumsy, out-of-shape athlete with a bad attitude, but an athlete nonetheless.

In the months that followed, I was cruelly sweet-talked, cajoled, and made to feel like a sex goddess every time I dragged my carcass back into the apartment.

By the end of the year, the honeymoon was over. I was a runner. No more sweet talk. We hammered out budget problems while doing the five-mile loop around Central Park. But by then it didn't matter, because I was hooked.

I never did learn to run very fast, but I did my halfhearted best and actually completed the 1992 New York City Marathon, which was something I never thought I would be stupid enough to attempt. I limped across the finish line, accepted the rose and medal they gave everyone who managed to finish that 26.2-mile death march, and burst into tears.

The following year, my knees gave out. I returned to my old

spot on the sofa and played the veteran athlete. After all, I was cool. I had a sports injury.

Time passed, I entered menopause, and my gynecologist told me I had bigger problems than creaky knees. I was a candidate for osteoporosis and coronary artery disease. Osteoporosis? Heart attack? *Widow's hump? Hip fractures? You talkin' to me?* I was not comforted by the alternatives: low-impact aerobics, weight-training, treadmill. *Doc, say it ain't so. Hell, no, I won't go! I paid my dues. I got the war wounds to prove it.*

My jock-in-shining-armor stepped in, this time with a birthday gift of a personal trainer. More or less out of terror, I trained myself to wake with the sun (and the rain and the snow and the icy blasts from the Arctic Circle) to pick up lumps of cold iron and run nowhere fast on a strip of moving rubber.

Do I love it? Are you kidding? But I've created my little rituals—lightly buttered roll and coffee at the corner deli, five minutes of weather report on the gym TV, a brief chat with my sisters in suffering, and then, off I go. I have pet names for some of the more interesting equipment: Cheese Grater (Leg Press), Dentist's Chair (Leg Extension), Orgasmatron (Prone Leg Curl), Flying Trapeze (Gravitron). I grunt mightily when I lifting forty-pound weights, and I'm tickled by the surprised look on my trainer's face when I do more push-ups than I could do the week before. Afterward, I walk down the street stinking like a jock, taking manly swigs from my water bottle. I spit in the street—*I ain't no lady. I'm an athlete.*

I forgot to mention the icing on the cake: my flat tummy when I slip into a skinny little sliver of a dress. Next to being told I'm adored, I suppose that's the best motivation of all.

Don't feel guilty if you hate to exercise—exercise anyway.

It's okay to curse before, during and after—exercise anyway.

Exercise. Your body will follow. Eventually so will your mind.

POINT TO PONDER

Weight training reduces the risk of osteoporosis in postmenopausal women.

The American College of Sports Medicine (ACSM) fitness guidelines recommend the following for healthy adults:

20–60 minutes of aerobic activity 3–5 days a week

and

20–30 minutes of strength training using light weights (1–12 pounds) 2–3 times a week

and

stretching exercises a minimum of 2–3 times a week.

YOU GOTTA HAVE A DREAM

What do you want to look like in six months? How do you want to feel? Think about what you want to achieve in the long run. Do you want to lose a couple of dress sizes? Develop your pectoral muscles by summer? Walk up a flight of stairs without feeling your heart trying to jump out of your throat? Do you want to calm down? Do you want to decrease your chances of getting osteoporosis? Want to attract a new significant other?

If your goal is to lose weight:

- The best exercises are repetitive motions, such as walking, bike riding, jogging.
- Surprisingly, swimming may not be the best exercise to start. People who are overweight are more buoyant than thin individuals, and their bodies don't need to work very hard in the water. So, they don't burn many calories.
- Try doing strength-training exercises, which build calorie-burning muscles.

If your goal is to prevent osteoporosis:

- Strength training is best, because exercises that put pressure on the bones stimulate the flow of calcium into the skeleton. Two or three sessions a week are ideal.

Strength training uses weights between 1 and 12 pounds. These exercises work the major muscle groups. Generally, you should be able to complete 10-12 repetitions of three sets of exercises. If you can't, it means the weight is too heavy.

If your goal is aerobic fitness:

- You want to do exercises that push your heart rate to at least 55 to 65 percent of its maximum. Try brisk walking, jogging, cycling or a treadmill.

If your goal is to reduce stress:

- Try yoga, aerobics or tai chi.

Your goal is to become stronger and healthier. Please don't
kill yourself with good intentions. Get a physical checkup
before starting an exercise program.

POINT TO PONDER
Expectation tends to be self-fulfilling.
—Anonymous

TEMPUS FUGIT

You don't have to redo your schedule to start an exercise program.
Think seriously about the small pockets of free time you have. Be
flexible, but plan an exercise schedule that works. A half-hour,
three days a week, will work miracles.

SHORT-TERM GOALS

If you're a size 12 and your goal is to be a size 6, it's unrealistic to
expect that you'll reach your goal in six weeks. Wishing will not
make it happen. It's also not sensible to make short-term goals of
a drop in size every two weeks. You're setting yourself up for fail-
ure. You need to figure out conservative short-term goals that will
get you to the finish line.

When you start to exercise, you'll see immediate short-term
results, and then you'll reach a plateau. When you plateau,
adjust your goal so it reflects the reality. When you reach a
plateau, your goal might be to keep the gains you've made. Stick
with the program even when you're not seeing results. When
your body starts to register your efforts again, make another

goal. Until it does, your goal is to maintain the progress you've already made.

Example 1

   Long-term goal: To run 2 miles without getting winded

   Short-term goal: To run .5 mile without getting winded

   GAME PLAN:

   Week 1: Treadmill 5 minutes 3 times a week

            Walk .5 mile 3 times a week

   Week 2: Treadmill 5 minutes

            Walk and run .5 mile

   Week 3: Treadmill 10 minutes

            Run .5 mile

   Week 4: Assess comfort level at .5 run

            Maintain this level until you can run without

            becoming winded.

   What's your next short-term goal?

Example 2

   Long-term goal: To become aerobically fit

   Week 1 Goal:

   • To make a commitment with a friend who has a similar goal
     and set up a serious, realistic schedule

   • To walk briskly for 20 minutes 3 times a week during the first
     2 weeks

   Week 3 Goal:

   • To maintain my walking schedule

   • To add 10 minutes on a bike or treadmill

Week 5 Goal:

- To walk 20 minutes 3 times a week

- To increase my bike/treadmill time to 20 minutes

- To assess my progress: How am I doing? Do I want to maintain this level of exercise?

    If I want to increase it, select Week 7 Goal (A)

    If I want to maintain my current level, select Goal (B)

Week 7 Goal (A):

- To walk 20 minutes 3 times a week

- To increase my time on the bike or treadmill to 30 minutes

or

Week 7 Goal (B):

- To maintain my current level of activity for another 2 weeks

SELF EXAMINATION TEST

- Long-term goal: In six months I want to achieve:
- How much time can I reasonably devote every day?

  (Mark a "0" on the days you don't plan to exercise.)

  Monday: ___ Tuesday: ___ Wednesday: ___ Thursday: ___

  Friday: ___ Saturday: ___ Sunday: ___

- What exercise do I want to do? (See page 53.)
- I want to achieve the following short-term goals:

  Week 1:

  Game Plan:

  Week 3:

  Game Plan:

  Week 5:

  Game Plan:

  Week 7:

  Game Plan:

Reaching your goal doesn't happen overnight, and it's not easy. The first step is to understand that it takes time to develop an exercise habit. Most of us are sloths at heart, just as most of us are cowards who would prefer not to visit the dentist, take flu shots, or agree to some of the more obnoxious invasive procedures we endure in the name of health. *Don't give up when you seem to be failing.* Give yourself credit for trying. Analyze why you missed the mark. Don't get global. It doesn't help to say, "I never *ever* could exercise." Instead, be specific. If you've slept through the alarm clock that you set to get up a half-hour early so you could work out, think of your options. For example, you could:

- Buy a louder alarm clock.
- Arrange to exercise with a friend/spouse/significant other who'll drag you out of bed.
- Find another time to exercise.

The only option you don't want to give yourself is the option to quit.

POINT TO PONDER
Walking is the best possible exercise.
—Thomas Jefferson

MOTIVATION

We asked our friends what they do about exercising and discovered that the answers are as individual as thumbprints. They all have personal ways of keeping fit and strategies to keep from giving up. They have their own goals and dreams and disappointments. The people we interviewed aren't athletes. For them, exercise is a challenge and a struggle. They gave us interesting insights into the motivation that ignites them, their observations and their efforts to get beyond the mental and physical hurdles.

Not one person said exercising wasn't worth the effort, and nobody said it was easy.

➤ I have this love-hate relationship with exercise. My

mother is kind of sedentary and my dad is not really sure what he wants to do.

I think what's keeping me from exercise is a psychological issue. It's just weird! I think it's tied to keeping my baby fat because that's what keeps me attached, it keeps me "baby." If all of a sudden I lost the weight I wanted to and got out there and really lived, I would be really separated from my family and on some level that still gives me anxiety. But I'm working on it.

I do have that desire to go out and be active, and I always feel better when I do. I'm starting to win, and I feel like I'm turning the corner, which is good, because I'm forty-four and it's about time!

—Bernice, age forty-four

Your Exercise Profile

A. History

1. Did you exercise as a kid? ☐ Yes ☐ No

   If yes, what exercise(s)?

2. Is there a sport you wish you had participated in but didn't?

3. Did anyone in your family exercise? ☐ Yes ☐ No

   If yes, what exercise(s)?

4. What message did your parents give you about exercise?

5. Did you exercise as a teenager? ☐ Yes ☐ No

   If yes, what exercise(s)?

↝ Starting at twenty-one, I began doing weight training and calisthenics and then at around thirty I started aerobic exercise. Right now I do a combination of walking and jogging. I try to increase my jogging as much as possible over the weeks and months—it all adds up to a limit of forty minutes a day. I'd like to exercise five times a week, but most weeks it's three times because of my schedule.

To keep motivated, it's mostly that I know exercise is one of the few things that will really work to raise my "good" cholesterol—my HDL. I also stay motivated by the desire to look good, and I say to myself, I really need to stay in good shape and have my maximum energy.

—Peter, age fifty-five

Your Exercise Profile

B. Physical Activity

1. Do you exercise? (Brisk walking counts as an exercise.)

   ☐ Yes ☐ No

   Details

2. How often do you exercise?

   ☐ Weekly ☐ Daily ☐ Sometimes

   Details:

3. What's the next level to which you'd like to take your exercise?

   ☐ I'd like to begin

   ☐ I'd like to advance

   ☐ I'd like to maintain my current level

   Details:

4. Do you belong to a gym? □ Yes □ No

5. Is there an activity you would like to try but are too self-conscious or embarrassed to start? □ Yes □ No
Details:

POINT TO PONDER
Drinking a sixteen-ounce bottle of water is an easy
way to look like a jock.

CHOOSING A HEALTH CLUB

Health clubs are personal. Some people are energized by a high-profile club that provides amenities such as a cappuccino bar and piped-in music. They enjoy dressing up in chic exercise gear and being part of a group dynamic. For others, it's intimidating and a waste of money.

Judith joined a fancy gym with a fancy price tag and went exactly twice all year. Later, she discovered a YWCA near our home that offers everything at a reasonable price. It's down-to-earth and quiet, and even exercise-adverse Judith feels comfortable. Before you shell out hundreds of dollars for a health club, ask yourself the following questions.

- Is the gym accessible? If you're trying to begin a workout program, choose a facility that's near home. It's easier to find an excuse not to go if you have to spend a lot of time getting there.
- Does the gym offer programs that fit your level of proficiency? Don't be taken in by slick advertising. Remember, it

doesn't matter how high tech the equipment is if you're too weak or intimidated to use it.

- Do you feel comfortable at the club? Could you imagine dropping by if you had an hour to kill?
- Will you have to buy a new wardrobe to feel comfortable there? If so, is that something you want to have to do? Again, for some people it provides an added incentive, and for others it's an excuse not to go. "I haven't a thing to wear" shouldn't apply to your workout clothes.
- Does the gym have a month-by-month or other short-term membership plan? Is it flexible? Health clubs make a lot of money by signing up the "New Year's Resolution" crowd. Alas, you cannot bribe your body by forking over two thousand dollars and never using the facilities.

POINT TO PONDER

Walking is an excellent exercise. At fifty-five, my grandmother began walking five miles a day. She's now one hundred—and we have no idea where she is.

—Robert B. Reich

❧ I did not exercise as a teenager. I began exercising in earnest when I gave birth to my second child, twenty-one years ago, at age thirty-two. Today I am a dedicated runner. I jog four to five times a week and completed my first New York City Marathon in 1998.

I like being thin and being able to eat a lot and never having to watch calories. Vanity plays a role here—I like the results of running—a more youthful, energetic and thinner me.

—*Barbara, age fifty-three*

Your Exercise Profile

C. Vanity Impact

1. How do you like the way you look?
2. How do your clothes fit?
3. What do you like most about your body?
4. What do you like least about your body?
5. Taking into account the basic body type you have, what would your ideal body look like?

❧ I certainly used to be more active than I am now, but I do try. I try to walk at least two or three times a week. And I dance once a week for a couple of hours. I think my friend and I spur each other on. I wouldn't walk on my own.

—*Michele, age fifty-four*

❧ I think it would be great to exercise with other people; I would feel more comfortable and not so self-conscious. I think it would definitely help to motivate me.

Actually I have a gym in this building, and I use the treadmill from time to time—I have all this equipment right downstairs—I'm crazy, I don't know why I'm not using it more often. But there are mirrors, and I just hate it, I just hate looking at myself right now. Talk about poor self-image!

—*Yvonne, age forty-six*

MIRROR, MIRROR ON THE WALL,
ARE YOU PART OF MY DOWNFALL?

For goodness' sake, don't look in the mirror when you exercise. It's a surefire way to become discouraged. Here's the catch-22:

- I can't stand the way I look.
- I'm exercising so I can stand the way I look.
- I can't stand the way I look when I exercise.

Muscle tissue needs more calories to sustain itself than an equivalent amount of fat. The more developed your muscles are, the more you can eat without gaining weight.

Your Exercise Profile

D. Rituals

1. Do you have a person/people with whom you like to exercise?

2. Do you have a special place you enjoy exercising?

3. Do you have activities you like to do before and after your exercise?

4. Do you have special clothes you like to wear—clothes that are particularly comfortable or make you feel: Sexy? Athletic? Fit?

5. Do you have foods you like to eat before or after exercise?

A SPOONFUL OF SUGAR

You've got to have a gimmick. If you were raised in a household where physical activities were as habitual as brushing your teeth, you can skip this section.

For people who were raised in homes where a walk around the block was considered strenuous activity, it helps to have pleasurable activities to go along with the exercise—they act as positive reinforcement.

Make exercise part of your life by surrounding it with pleasant experiences. Coat your agony with sugar. Here are some suggestions to get you started.

- Exercise with someone you really like, or form an exercise group with some friends who are also trying to begin an exercise routine. Make it a social occasion.
- If you're going alone to a health club, get to know some people there. It's more fun to exercise with people you know, and you'll give each other support when the going gets rough.
- Even if you don't like to listen to music when you exercise, listen to a few moments of energizing music before you begin to get you in the mood.

- Treat yourself to a low-calorie dessert at the end of each workout. Make it a ritual.
- Treat yourself to a massage. It's good for sore muscles, and you'll love the way you feel afterward.
- Buy yourself a gift when you reach a goal.

Save one article of clothing to represent you at your most out of shape and/or overweight. Try it on when you reach a plateau and need a lift. It will remind you how far you've come.

DIVERSIFY

If you're easily bored, be versatile! Make a wish list of all the activities you'd like to do. List a friend or colleague with whom you'd like to share the activity. Figure out a realistic game plan for yourself. For example, if your list includes swimming, ice skating, bike riding and jogging, you might plan to swim in the summer, bike ride in the spring, and ice skate in the winter. You might choose to jog as a maintenance exercise but not to push yourself beyond your comfort zone.

⟣ What motivates me? I have periodic conversations with Death. I figure if I can keep in good trim, he'll think I'm young and basically avoid me for a while.

—Gregory, age forty-one

⟣ I go to the gym five days a week. My motivation is to look young. I always try to carve out time before or after work. I hate the thought of letting my body go. I hate the thought of getting older, so I exercise because of the illusion that it will keep me young. In my mind, I think I'm about twenty-five. I really do.

—Helene, age forty-six

Start slowly! Commit to thirty minutes twice a week for the first couple of weeks. Work the time up slowly.

CONFESSIONS OF AN EXERCISE NUT
by Steve Estrine

I was such a fat kid that physical exercise was nearly impossible. I remember standing outside the schoolyard gate watching the other kids play stickball and crying because I was too fat to climb over the gate and join them.

In high-school gym class, we had to climb a rope to the ceiling. I was so obese I couldn't get my legs around the rope. Besides, I had no upper-body strength, so there was no way I could haul my cargo up that rope. And to make matters worse, I was terrified of heights. I was afraid that if I managed to get up there, I'd come crashing down and kill myself. It was a humiliating experience.

When I was a sophomore I developed a blood clot in my brain, and they rushed me to the hospital. Two holes were drilled in my cranium, and my equilibrium was permanently shot. But it got me out of gym. I was thirteen at the time, and I remember thinking that they could drill as many holes as they wanted as long as I didn't have to climb that rope. In college I took swimming and hated every moment of it.

After I completed all the compulsory gym classes I'd ever have to take, I avoided exercise like the plague until I was thirty, when my doctor convinced me to join a local Y.

I tried playing basketball and volleyball, but I had poor equilibrium as a result of the brain surgery. Then I tried indoor track. Bliss. I didn't have to climb ropes, freeze in a pool, or embarrass myself on the court. All I had to do was move my feet.

I'd get on the track, and there would be these attractive women runners, and I'd run behind them. After a while, I could keep up with the faster runners. It felt great. One day I realized I was running a mile, and that was good. I stayed at a mile for about a year and then discovered I could run two miles. When I looked back to where I had started, it was a major accomplishment.

One day, it occurred to me that since I had gone from a quarter of a mile to two miles, I might actually make it to four. And since there were always new women coming to the track, it kept me going like a little rabbit.

Today I can say (with some amazement and a touch of pride) that I'm an athlete. I'm a man in my fifties with two holes in my head and an equilibrium problem that keeps me from riding a bicycle or playing hopscotch with my daughter. I can't swim and I won't go near a basketball. But I can run.

When I turned fifty, I saw a group of New York City marathoners limping home, and I said to myself, I can do that. But when I thought about actually running twenty-six miles I became terrified. I imagined my mother saying, Are you crazy? You want to drop dead?

I convinced Judith to run the marathon with me. I figured if I had a heart attack, she could get me to a hospital. It was a nice run, I didn't die, and since then I've run seven marathons. My goal is to become the oldest marathon runner in America. I want to be 120 years old and run in the Marine Corps Marathon. I want to be the poster boy for the 100 plus generation.

Recommended Reading

Strength Basics: Your Guide to Resistance Training for Health and Optimal Performance, by Brian B. Cook, Gordon W. Stewart, Human Kinetics, 1996

Strength Training Past 50, by Wayne L. Westcott, Mark Williams, Thomas Baechie, Human Kinetics, 199.

Strong Women Stay Young, by Miriam E. Nelson, Susan Wernick, Bantam Books, 1997

Weight Training for Dummies, by Liz Neporent, Suzanne Schlosberg. IDG Books Worldwide, 1997

Newsletters

Harvard Health Letter
P.O. Box 380
Boston, MA 02117
617-432-1485
Web site: http://www.harvardhealthpubs.org/Harvard_Search

Focus on Healthy Aging
Mt. Sinai Medical Center
P.O. Box 420235
Palm Coast, FL 32142-0235
800-829-9406

Consumers Report
101 Truman Ave.
Yonkers, NY 10703-1057
914-378-2000

The United Kingdom
Resources

Health-club.net
0870 160 5555
Provides a directory of health, sports and leisure clubs, including gyms, aerobics, fitness classes, swimming pools, etc.
http://www.health-club.net.

FOUR

Our Aging Parents

> ### POINT TO PONDER
> "It's not fair. My mother wasn't supposed to get old.
> She wasn't supposed to need me. It's just like her to change the
> rules just when I was starting to get our relationship right!"
> —Conversation overheard on a bus

Overnight, it seems, our parents are becoming old. They need us in ways we never asked to be needed. In a strange reversal of roles, we find ourselves worrying about them. We're called upon to make decisions about things we've never even thought about before. Suddenly, we understand that our parents are not immortal. And that means neither are we.

✦ When my mother was in the hospital we took walks together. We used to be about the same height. All of a sudden she's six inches shorter than I am and I'm holding her hand like a little girl.

—*Michele, age fifty-four*

This new dimension in our lives takes some getting used to. With the exception of people who are professional caregivers, being a parent is the closest most of us have ever come to the experience of being responsible for another person. But our parents aren't kids—not ours or anyone else's. They're adults who will need assistance to varying degrees as they age.

Ever notice how comedians rummage through the darkest corners of their families' lives for material? They amuse us with their stories of relationships run amuck, and we shriek with laughter. Why? Because we can relate—from a comfortable distance. Secretly, each of us knows by heart the lyrics to our own family's looney tunes. Each parent-child relationship is unique, and depending on the kind of relationship you have with your parents, they will either come forward and ask for assistance, wait for you to figure out what they need, or deny they need help at all. It becomes your responsibility to know what's going on in their lives.

⁌ They became more frail but they made it seem like everything else was fine. My sister and I found out afterward that there was a shortage of money, and my father wasn't getting enough food. . . . I don't know if it was malnutrition, but almost at the very end, we found out he was upset that my mother cut down on portions for him because of money. And he didn't tell me until the very end.

Also, even though we got them someone who cleaned the apartment every couple of weeks, right after my father died I spent some time at the house. I noticed my mother wasn't sealing bags of cookies well and roaches were running around. It was clear that they weren't functioning *nearly* as well as they pretended.

I don't know if we could have done anything different. They were very difficult people. We spoke to them on the phone a lot, but visits were minimal. If we had spent a lot of time with them at the house we would have begun to see what was going on. But they didn't encourage us, they didn't say they needed anything, and they kept us at arm's length. They were covering up a lot of things, like the amount of money they had and the way the house was being kept up. A whole lot of stuff.

—*Peter, age fifty-five*

HOW DO YOU GET THE
COMMUNICATION BALL ROLLING?

You've been leading your own life and practicing benign neglect, but now it's time to get involved. Here are some suggestions to get started:

- Call once a week even if you stay on the phone for one minute. Make it a ritual.
- Gossip about someone you all dislike—family, friends,

political figures, movie stars—anyone. It takes the heat off you, and its a great bonding tool.

- Get your parents hooked up to e-mail. Make sure you're on-line too. E-mail them every day—it doesn't have to be long—just a sign that you're thinking of them. Be specific. Ask them what they've had for lunch, what they're watching on television, how they're feeling. Tell them something about your day. It doesn't have to be profound. It can be as trite as, "My bird doesn't like the seeds I've bought him" or "Can't find a decent dress that fits" or "The kids have the flu. Gotta run."

- Make a date to go to a restaurant. If your parent has trouble with vision, make sure the restaurant is well lit. If your parent has difficulty walking, make sure the rest rooms are on the same floor as the dining area and that the restaurant is on street level.

- Reminisce about old times while enjoying old family pictures. Keep it *real* old to avoid bringing up present-day conflicts.

- Buy something they need but won't ask for.

- Send mail—pictures, postcards, a funny newspaper or magazine article.

- If you live nearby, check in often—even if only for a few minutes. If you live far away, get the telephone number of a friend or neighbor of your parent and establish a phone relationship. Encourage this contact to keep you abreast of any changes that occur in your parent's status and to call you in an emergency.

- If you have had a long-standing feud or misunderstanding

with your parents, try to swallow your pride and make peace. Life is too short to carry around baggage this heavy!

- Ask them for help or advice in an area you know they can still help. Think about how you can make it a victory for them.

Remember, you can't know what your parents are thinking and what they need and want until you make yourself available. Your parents won't be able to tell you unless they know you're listening. Talk to them! Listen to what they have to say.

⚜ I go to Florida once a year and spend a few boring days poolside. My parents are very independent. I go because I'm guilty. At some point in time I will probably have to make certain decisions for them. I've come to terms with this.

There are moments where my mother can still "zing it" to me. That part has not changed. But I think I'm able to cope with it a little bit better now that I'm older. They were in a car accident down in Florida, and I stayed with them for a while. It was strange all of a sudden to realize that these people who held so much power over me, both physically and emotionally, were totally dependent on me.

—*Olivia, age forty-six*

⚜ The signs of aging in my parents . . . that's complicated. My mother's health has broken down, and she is fragile now. She didn't use to be. My father is physically robust, but he's emotionally crankier than before.

I'm a lesbian, and I think I have a unique role among my siblings in that I've never gone to my parents with my problems. We were either on the outs, or what I was doing was something they would totally advise me against. So I've never been in the role of waiting for advice, and I also haven't burdened them with my problems.

As a result, I find that my mother seems to use me as a confidante in ways that she's not using my other siblings. She can complain to me about my father, and she can confide some of her worries. She knows I'm not going to get too upset. I think she has confidence in my judgment. And I feel she gets comfort just out of being able to confide in me, and that's the way it is most of the time. I'm allowing her to take comfort in confiding the way another person would go to a therapist and just talk.

—*Maggie, age forty-nine*

HOW CAN YOU HELP YOUR PARENTS RETOOL?

POINT TO PONDER
Age is opportunity no less
Than youth itself, though in another dress.

—Henry Wadsworth Longfellow
Morituri Salutamus

Your parents may need your encouragement to shift gears. They may be embarrassed or lack the confidence to admit that, in their heart of hearts, they want to join a gym or oil paint or take a course in French literature. They may not know about opportunities for continuing education in their community or venues that exist for teaching younger people some of the skills they've amassed over years of experience. They may need the encouragement of a supportive younger person. You.

* * *

Steve was born very late in his mother's life, and she died when he was only thirty-six. She was bright, ambitious and very competitive, but she couldn't go to college when she was young. So, after retiring, she took college courses. Steve was in graduate school in Utah, and he'd get jubilant letters from her, saying things like, "I got an A in English—if memory serves, you only got a B."

She died peacefully in her sleep at the age of seventy-nine, secure in the knowledge that her son might have his doctorate, but she was a better student.

Help your parents retool for the next stage of life. Help them access community resources for older persons. For example:

- A local Y
- A church or synagogue
- A volunteer program in a school or hospital
- A health club (sometimes clubs have big discounts for people over sixty-five).

Help your parents reach out to national organizations whose function it is to empower older people to enjoy life to the hilt. (See Resources.)

AUTUMN OF LOVE

Here's some shocking news: 10 percent of all reported cases of AIDS in this country occur in persons over sixty-five, and there is a rise in AIDS among older women. The silver lining to this terrible cloud is that it proves beyond a shadow of a doubt that older persons are enjoying sex in their seventies, eighties and beyond. Another fantasy about old age bites the dust. Now we'll all have to accept that our parents may be happily pitching woo.

If you're looking at nursing facilities for your parents, inquire whether they have private accommodations for couples. Homes that don't get federal funding aren't legally required to respect the privacy of their residents, and married couples can be housed in separate wings. The assumption is that old people just don't care about love and sex anymore.

If your mom or dad lives alone, there's a chance they may be having sex with one or more partners. If you know your parent has more than one sexual partner, or if your father is paying for sex, please find a way to get information to him or her about the importance of safe sex.

Occasionally, your parent may feel sufficiently desperate to discuss a sexual problem with you. Take it as a compliment that you're trusted, but don't feel you have to play Dr. Ruth Westheimer. Treat the information confidentially and respectfully. Admit to feeling awkward and offer to help find a geriatrician who can listen and sensitively offer medical or psychological alternatives.

In their illuminating book *Love and Sex After Sixty*, Robert N. Butler, M.D., and Myrna Lewis, M.S.W., discuss the medical and psychosocial challenges of sexual love in the later years of life. Read it, and if you feel it's appropriate, share the book with your parent.

Imagine yourself at seventy-eight: healthy, energetic and eager to keep enjoying a robust libido. The baby-boomer generation created the Summer of Love. Maybe we are hopeless romantics, but we believe that the Autumn of Love can be as exciting and, in its own way, as fulfilling.

NUTS AND BOLTS

When your parents become frail, it's sometimes difficult to know what to do. We asked two physicians who specialize in care for the aging to speak to the important issues that confront the children of older parents.

Linda Brady, M.D., is medical director and director of neurology and psychiatry at Kingsbrook Jewish Medical Center in Brooklyn, New York. Gabe Koz, M.D., is a clinical professor of psychiatry at New York University School of Medicine.

How do we assess our parent's ability to continue to live independently, and how can we help them remain independent?
First of all, do it with love. People bring a lot of baggage from past relationships with them. If there is love and concern, children will find a way to assist their parents.

1. You need to be aware if a significant loss of weight or a change in appetite has occurred.

A loss of weight alerts you to a number of possibilities.

- Are your parent's teeth in poor condition so they're just not able to chew and eat in the same way?
- Is your parent depressed?
- Does he/she have some dietary restriction that makes the food bland? If that's the case, you may need to look for a salt substitute to jazz it up.
- Taste buds and sense of smell change with time, and older people can find eating less pleasurable.
- You need to examine whether there has been a change in the way meals are prepared. For example, if your parent is a surviving spouse and the partner was the one who cooked, the survivor may not be able to prepare meals.
- Are there physical or mental limitations that hamper your parent's ability to prepare his or her own food? (A woman we know who used to do lots of cooking became forgetful. She would cook and leave out ingredients so the food tasted horrible, and she wouldn't eat it.)

SUGGESTIONS

- Get "Meals on Wheels," or arrange for the local deli to deliver several meals a week.
- Make sure your parent has enough money to eat out.
- Make sure the refrigerator is stocked. Ask family members to come bearing care packages when they visit. Parents may say, "Oh, how can you bring me so much? I can't eat all this stuff," but it all goes into the freezer, and somehow it gets eaten.

- Bring in the "troops" to keep an eye on things. Social support in the form of a son or daughter dropping in to say "hi" or share a meal and make sure a parent eats goes a long way, and it's also a good way for the child to check up on things.

2. *Look at your parent's ability to move about in the home environment. Does the physical setup present problems?*
   - Does your parent have difficulty negotiating the stairs?
   - Is the bathroom accessible?
   - Is the laundry room in the basement? Are the steps hazardous?
   - If your parent lives in a private house, are the bathroom and bedroom on the same floor?

SUGGESTIONS
   - Small pieces of furniture, such as coffee tables and end tables, are homey but hazardous, since they are easy to trip over.
   - Carpeting and runners must be securely tacked down.
   - It also helps to have places throughout the house where an older person can rest. For example, if you place a chair near the bed, your parent can sit down to put on socks. For some elderly people, putting on socks while they stand is nearly impossible.
   - Check where your parent keeps clothes and other items. Does your mom or dad have to stretch? Lift? Bend? Think of ways you can compensate for physical limitations.
   - If you parent is receptive, you can have someone come in to do light cleaning and shopping.

3. Loss of vision

You have to be observant. Is your parent:

- Squinting?
- Not reading as much?
- Bumping into things or tripping over them?
- Depth perception is also a factor. It can't easily be corrected with glasses but nevertheless has to be taken into consideration when someone is falling a lot.

SUGGESTION

- Assist your mom or dad in getting an eye exam and help arrange for corrective lenses.

4. Memory loss

Forgetfulness becomes unacceptable when it starts to interfere with your parent's ability to function. Clearly, if you don't live in the house and are far away, it's that much harder to assess the situation. You really need to visit and observe your parent pretty regularly to be able to determine if memory loss is a problem.

For example, if you're trying to assess your mom's status, you have to ask:

- Is she clean?
- How is she dressing? Does it seem appropriate?
- Is she putting her clothes on the way she always has and does she look as well kept as she always was?
- What does the house look like?
- Are pots burnt because she's forgotten to shut off the burner?

- Has she gotten lost?
- Have neighbors reported that she goes out and forgets her keys and/or leaves the door open?

These are the signs that should really worry you as far as safety and impaired functioning are concerned.

5. Lifestyle changes

It's normal for lifestyles to change throughout our lives. As we get older, things slow down, and our interests change. You can't bring your own values to bear, and you need to have a degree of tolerance.

People say, "My mother used to be fun-loving, running around trying everything, now she's slowing down and looking inward." That's not necessarily bad. The parameters must be broad, and you must allow your parents to change and develop in different ways than you may want.

By and large, children need to work to achieve a level of acceptance. We need to take into account our own feelings about what we see. But we also have to make allowances for the changes aging brings about.

POINT TO PONDER

Things do not change; we change.

—Henry David Thoreau
Walden

What about driving?

Driving is a symbol of independence, autonomy, adulthood. It's painful to have to take it away, but safety must take precedence. Be alert to little fender-bender driving accidents that happen more than you would expect. Understand that you're in a very tough position. There's no easy way around it.

Most states require 20/40 vision in one eye for an unrestricted driver's license. Some states allow residents with limited vision to drive with a restricted license, that is, driving on local streets or driving that is restricted to the daylight hours. Call your secretary of state's office to find out the laws in your state.

SUGGESTIONS

- Sit down and try to negotiate with your parent.
- Try to involve the family doctor. The doctor is an authority figure. A physician's opinion, as opposed to that of a daughter or son, can be perceived as objective.
- Unfortunately, you may eventually have to take away the car keys.

To make up for this loss, be creative.

- If finances allow, establish a charge account for your parent with the local taxi service, so that transportation is available if he or she wants to shop, go to the movies or visit friends.
- Look into transportation available through senior citizen centers in your parent's neighborhood.
- Arrange for friends, neighbors or family members who live in the neighborhood to provide support. You might help out with gas money if it's appropriate.

If your parent is legally blind she/he may be eligible for a federal tax exemption. Legal blindness means that your parent's best corrected vision is not better than 20/200 in either eye and that the visual field is 20 degrees or less. See your optometrist or ophthalmologist for documentation of legal blindness.

How do we determine if our parent needs some form of supervision in the home? What options do we have?

The wonderful standard that is applied in law, and in psychiatry as well, is that everybody, whether mentally ill or experiencing a change in functioning, should be in the least restricted environment necessary to be comfortable and safe—and hopefully, happy.

Of course, judgments have to be made, and when that happens, courts, judges and society tend to err on the side of trying to give people as much freedom as possible. Yet the day comes when a person's inability to function adequately declares itself to the community or to the family. A person may begin wandering around at night or be unable to keep clean or remain properly nourished. Then personal safety becomes a concern.

1. Physical Assistance

Most people really do want to remain in their homes, and ways exist to help your parent maintain a reasonable degree of independence while assuring her/his safety. Your parent may need to be watched more closely.

- You can arrange for supervision, either periodic outside supervision, such as a handyman or someone to do some light cleaning, or a family member who drops in on a regular basis to see that your mom or dad is eating properly and is clean and dressed.

- Your parent can remain at home with some kind of in-house support. This support can range from a home health aide who attends to your parent for a couple of hours a day to a full-time aide who lives with your parent.

2. Emotional Status

Another factor to consider is your parent's psychological status.

- If warning signs appear, it's time to ask for outside opinions. People who see your mom or dad frequently are in a position to observe if something is amiss.

- If serious concerns are raised, these should be brought to the attention of a primary care physician who has experience working with aging individuals. The doctor will assess your parent and rule out a multitude of possibilities. A physical illness, such as hypertension and diabetes, can cause mental deterioration. If the illness is properly diagnosed and treated, your parent may return to a higher level of functioning.

- If your parent is very depressed or feeling hopeless, it is important to get a mental status assessment. A social worker or psychologist is a good place to start. But if the emotional distress becomes very severe and your parent needs medication, you'll need a psychiatric consultation.

What factors do we have to weigh when we consider having a parent live with us?

Parents moving in with their children is a complicated and very emotional issue. Here are some of the points that need to be considered before making a move:

- Parent and child must be equally eager for this arrangement.
- The new living arrangement must have a degree of familiarity and comfort for the parent.
- How is this new arrangement going to impact on your parent? You may be removing a person from a familiar location and from long-standing friends and relationships. It represents a major social change. Now your parent becomes totally dependent on you and your family. It really changes the equation.
- How long will you be able to sustain the arrangement? Can you do it for ten years or longer? You have to understand you're in it for the long haul. Once your parent makes the move, it's going to be very hard to undo.
- Are you prepared to handle a change in the functional status of your parent?
- What kind of relationship do you have with your parent? Will your family history color your decisions and influence your behavior? Are you prepared to deal with painful parent/child issues that may crop up?
- How is your parent moving in going to affect your relationship with your spouse and kids? They may experience your increased attentiveness to your parent as their loss. In these

situations, it is natural that they may eventually have negative things to say about this accommodation. It's important that you and your family recognize the existence of such negative feelings and establish ways to address and resolve them on an ongoing basis.

❧ Differentiate what you or your siblings think is best versus what your parent really wants. Hear and listen and pay attention to what your parent is saying, because if you don't, it can really be a disaster.

—*Linda Brady, M.D.*

❧ We grew up in the slums of New York City—Hell's Kitchen. I couldn't wait to get out, but the neighborhood was all my mother knew.

My sister and I very much wanted Mom to move in with my sister in the suburbs. We knew we would feel better, that it would be safer and we wouldn't have to worry about her, but she felt like she would die if she went to the suburbs. She said she would feel isolated not having access to transportation the way she had in the city. She knew she would be totally dependent on my sister for transportation. She was accustomed to all the action in the city. She told us she would be more frightened in the suburbs.

We thought it would be best for her, but thankfully we had the sense not to force it. Looking back, I think it would have been easier for us, but I'm glad Mom held her ground. I'm glad we didn't try to wear her down.

—*Barbara, age forty-six*

❧ There is no advice you can give about letting a parent move in. Family dynamics skew the equation and a lot depends on the culture and the individuals who are involved. Some people say, "No problem" to having a family member live with them and in some cultures it's the natural, normal thing. But in our society people say, "I can't handle this." And they won't.

—Gabriel Koz, M.D.

❧ I'd open a vein before letting my mother invade my life. It would be an assault.

—Esther, age forty-four

❧ They'd never come to live with me. When the time comes, Mom and Dad will go to a nursing home together.

—Jay, age forty-four

❧ I could see my mother moving in. Would I be happy? I don't know. I think my wife would be upset, and we'd have to work it out. But I couldn't say no, and yeah, I guess we have the room.

—Jerome, age fifty-eight

❧ If one of them passed away, I could see the other one moving in with my sister. Not me. She's the one with the patience.

—Howie, age forty-seven

❧ I don't think my mother would be happy living with me,

and I don't think I could stand her depression. To tell the truth, I think she needs an environment with people around her. Could I get her to agree to go to a nursing home? Who knows.

—*Pattie, age forty-seven*

❧ When Dad reaches the point where he can't take care of himself, I think he'll simply die. I think it would kill him to be dependent.

—*Paul, age fifty-eight*

❧ After Dad died, Mom couldn't take care of herself and so my wife and I asked her to live with us. She was confused and became terrified in the middle of the night. We began to give up our own lives, even with full-time assistance. A year after she came, we couldn't go on, and my brother and I agreed to admit her to a nursing home. I'm still feeling guilty about it.

—*Donald, age fifty-eight*

❧ Dad came to live with us when I was forty-seven. For the first few months it was very strange because all of a sudden I was living with my "daddy" again. Also, here I was, the one female in the house between a husband and a father. I was very nervous trying to please both, and you can't always please everybody. There were times when I had arguments with Sam in the bedroom because I was very nervous, and for a while it affected our relationship. I was nervous because of the relationship that Sam had with

Dad. They didn't always get on well. They were both vying for my attention, and I was trying to give it to two people I loved.

There was always a little bit of tension in the house, and I was always working very hard to keep the two of them happy with each other.

It was a good thing that I worked part time and got to leave the house. And in a way it was good for Dad that Sam had his consulting business in the house. There was someone to be with Dad. Even though Sam was working, there was someone there. There were people who came to the house to talk to Sam about business, and that was good for Dad. I think eventually they sort of reached an armistice. They were at peace with each other.

My advice to anyone thinking of having their parent come live with them is that you have to have enough room for them so that you have some privacy. I was lucky to have a big enough house so he could be downstairs in his own room with his own bathroom and he could close the door.

And you have to have a very understanding spouse. I had a friend whose father moved near to where they lived, but the husband would not allow the father to move in with them, even though they had a big house. I have to give my husband credit: He welcomed my Dad, even though he got exasperated sometimes.

I think it was a good experience, although it's one I wouldn't have chosen. When he passed away there was a loss and a mourning, but I had ten years with him of which about seven were very, very good. I would say yes, if you can do it, it's good. It will leave you with memories you couldn't have any other way. You get married, and you leave your parents home. You may visit on Sundays, but living with them is different.

We had very good times together—in the summertime taking walks in the evening, sitting in the garden, going shopping. I mean, he could be exasperating like anyone is, but I have very fond memories.

In the long run, I had an old-fashioned feeling about my parents. That was the bottom line: He was my father.

—Rachel, age fifty-nine

What role should we play when our parent is hospitalized, and what should we look for to indicate our parent is receiving proper care?

If your parent is hospitalized, keep asking questions until you feel satisfied that you know what's wrong in layman's terms. If someone you know has medical knowledge, ask that person to accompany you when you speak to the physician.

- Ask what you can reasonably expect in terms of your parent's condition.
- What are the potential complications of the condition?
- Is there a risk of loss of competency during the hospitalization?
- What is the probability of your parent's returning home and to a prehospital level of functioning upon discharge?

These questions are important for a number of reasons. Families need to plan and make decisions. The earlier you can anticipate specific occurrences, the better. Often at the end of the hospitalization everything is thrown at you, and you don't really have time to prepare or to make sound decisions.

- Talk to the social worker about the social supports that might be necessary and available to your parent at different points, as well as possible benefits to which your parent is entitled.
- If your parent is going to be in the hospital for a long time, ask if physical therapy will be provided to keep muscle tone intact.
- Your parent must be encouraged to move out of bed as soon as possible.
- Your parent must be given assistance in walking to prevent falls.

It's very important to mobilize older hospital
patients and keep them moving and functioning.
They can go downhill very quickly.

- Pay visits at meal time to see if your parent can eat alone or needs to be fed.
- Help your parent fill out a menu.
- Be alert to loss of dentures, which can happen easily in a hospital setting.
- Ask staff about how well your parent is eating to see if they know what's going on.
- If your parent is not mobile, observe if he/she is in the same

position each time you visit. If a patient is not ambulatory, the physical position must be changed several times a day. Look for signs of redness on the back and/or buttocks, which is an indication of bedsores or the potential for bedsore formation.

- Is your parent clean?
- Is the environment clean?
- Press the call bell. Does someone respond in a timely manner? Is the bell accessible to the patient?
- Your parent should be relatively free of pain. If your parent is experiencing pain, is it being appropriately attended to?
- If you have questions about whether your parent is being properly cared for in the hospital, you can speak to the nursing supervisor, a patient-relations representative or a hospital administrator. Families are afraid if they complain, their parent will be punished, but that's highly unlikely. The higher you go up the chain of command, the less you have to be frightened of. People pay attention when supervisors and high-level administrators are served with complaints. If you really feel that the hospital is doing nothing about the situation, report it to your State Department of Health. This agency is required to investigate every patient complaint.

SPECIAL PROBLEMS OF THE AGED
IN A HOSPITAL SETTING

When older persons go into the hospital, they run the risk of the hospital staff not understanding their needs. Everything is attributed to, "Oh, well, it's old age," instead of understanding that it may be a matter of a confused state of mind or delirium. The hospital is a very difficult environment for older people.

- Unfamiliarity with the new environment creates the potential for your parent to become more confused. This is often compounded by the lack of good sleep in a hospital because of the noise, the lights and staff coming and going, and waking patients up to do tests and take blood.
- The risk for falls increases. An older person may try to get out of bed in the night to go to the bathroom, and the side rails may be up to prevent falls. When the nurse doesn't respond immediately to the call bell, the patient may try to climb over the rail and fall.
- Older persons can easily become disoriented in a hospital setting. You can help your parent by bringing a little clock or an inexpensive watch. It is also helpful to bring some small items from home that are familiar but that won't be missed if they get lost in the hospital.

What should we look for when we must choose a good nursing home for our parent?
Finding a good nursing home can be done by word of mouth, talking to families of people who are in nursing homes, and by visiting several homes.

- During your visit, observe the level of cleanliness. Do you detect a pervasive odor?
- Is the home bright?

- Is the staff friendly?
- Are the residents doing activities? Do they seem happy and occupied? Are they clean?
- When you walk around, how many residents are in bed? Are many just sitting in hallways unoccupied?
- Find out what the activity schedule looks like and what's really going on.
- Talk to residents of the home and the home's resident council. Attend resident council meetings because residents are usually very vocal about what their problems are. Talk to the head of the resident council.

Public information is another way to find a good nursing home. You can call the State Department of Health and check whether a particular home has had any violations or complaints against it.

Nursing homes do not have to be accredited in order to operate, but more and more of them are becoming accredited. You can call the Joint Commission of Accreditation of Hospitals, if the Joint Commission accredits the nursing home you're interested in.

Another resource is the Alzheimer's Association. (See Resources.)

You should also evaluate the physicians:

- Are they board certified?
- Are they salaried physicians who are on the premises for a number of hours, or are they voluntary physicians who come in, make rounds and leave, and are basically just on-call?
- How often will your parent get seen by a physician?

• What hospital will be used if your parent gets sick? How do you feel about that hospital?

What can we do to make our parent feel more at home in a supervised residence?

It takes from four to eight weeks for aging persons to adjust to a nursing home, and they can be quite miserable during that time. The way to help your parent deal with the shock and adjustment is by visiting often, especially at the beginning. It's a normal reaction to a massive change and to loss: the loss they are experiencing at the end of life, loss of their faculties, loss of their family, their home, their autonomy. They are grieving and mourning.

It is normal for people who enter a nursing home to be depressed, and it takes various forms. People who are resilient can be mildly depressed. Some people snap out of it in a week or two. Others never emerge. They go promptly into a deep clinical depression and need psychiatric treatment. Ultimately, most people adapt. They adapt to the home, to their room, to the staff, and eventually, they reach a plateau of acceptance and comfort.

Sometimes, perhaps a year later, the staff may decide they have to move your parent to a new room on a new floor. Don't be surprised if your parent goes through the same depression and the same adjustment reaction of moving to another floor or another room. People don't want change.

As a loving child, you can help your parent adjust to moving into a nursing home or adult residence. Try to make the new room as homelike as possible by moving in some pieces of familiar household items. Try to de-institutionalize your parent's space by bringing family pictures and bedspreads.

Somehow you need to let the staff know who your parent really is. Very often, by the time people go into nursing homes, they are just shells of the vibrant individuals they once were. Try and get the staff to know who your parent was in the world.

One nursing home has a videotape of every resident. It helps the staff become aware of who this person really is. Nursing home staff usually has no idea who the patients really are, what their relationships with their children are like, what they did for a living, what activities they enjoy or what their interests are.

It is also very important that you visit nursing homes before you decide which one to choose. Stay for lunch. Make an effort to get to know the surroundings and the staff. All of these steps will go a very long way in determining how your parent is treated. It will make a big difference in your parent's adjustment in the new environment.

⌁ We have to think of a way to take better care of each other when we get ancient! I know I definitely want to know what doctors are going to take care of me when I get older because people who are now being trained in medicine in this managed-care, technological environment don't know how to examine a person anymore.

My doctor is in his seventies; he spends an hour to an hour and a half with me, he knows how to do a physical exam, and he answers my questions. He doesn't wait until something shows up on a CAT scan, and it's too late. But I don't know long he'll be around. He told me that doctors and residents "in the old days" used to sit in the cafeteria and talk about medicine. Now they sit in the cafeteria and talk about the stock market.

—Gloria, age forty-five

⤚ My mother is in her ninth decade and she is in really great health. She lives in a retirement community in Florida, she's never been hospitalized, and she's very independent. She just called to tell me she wants a computer and that she's found a community college that gives introductory computer courses. She still drives, and she's signed up for this course. I'm thrilled.

—Ed, age forty-seven

⤚ During the years before my mother's death I think our relationship deepened and I learned a lot from her about courage. I saw her as she lost her vision gradually and lost her physical mobility. She became frail physically and that was the bottom line. Her mind was wonderful, almost to the end.

Gradually she began to need help at home. First someone came in three times a week for four hours a day and then it was five days a week, four hours a day, and then it increased and became a full day and then eventually she needed full-time at-home care.

I struggled with the idea of her living with me, but her needs were so great, and I needed to be able to get away from them for a while. I had trouble with that.

So, now I've experienced the loss of my mother, who I

loved dearly, and I'm an orphan. I'm trying to understand how she continues to live within me and how in my life I can continue to express her life. Kind of like an ever-flowering tree.

—Beverly, age fifty-seven

Recommended Reading

Caring For Your Aging Parents: A Planning and Action Guide, by Donna Carl Cohen & Eisendorf, J.P. Tarcher, 1995

Love and Sex After 60, by Robert N. Butler, M.D., Myrna I. Lewis, G.K. Hall & Co., 1996

Successful Aging: The MacArthur Foundation Study, by John W. Rowe, M.D., Robert L. Kahn, Ph.D., Pantheon, 1998

You and Your Aging Parents, by Barbara Silverstone, Helen Hyman, Pantheon Books, 1989

Resources—USA

AgeNet
644-A West Washington Avenue
Madison, WI 53703
www.agenet.com

Children of Aging Parents
800-227-7294

Eldercare Locator
800-677-1116

International Longevity Center
www.ilcusa.org

SeniorNet
Provides older adults with education for and access to
computer technology
121 Second Street - 7th floor
San Francisco, CA 94105
415-495-4990
www.seniornet.com

Social Security Administration
800-772-1213

American Association of Retired Persons (AARP)
601 E Street, NW
Washington, DC 20049
800-424-3410

Gray Panthers
165 West 86th Street
New York, NY
212-799-7572
Activist group of and for older people

Elderhostel
P.O. Box 1959
Dept XX1
Wakefield, MA 01880-5959
Educational programs for people over 55

Health-related Organizations

Alzheimer's Association
800-272-3900

The Arthritis Foundation
800-283-7800

American Heart Association
214-373-6300

The National Stroke Association
303-649-9299

National High Blood Pressure Education Program
301-592-8573

National Institute of Neurological Disorders and Stroke
800-352-9424

The United Kingdom
Resources

Age Concern is the center of a network of 1,100 autonomous local organizations that offer a wide range of community-based services.

Age Concern England
Astral House
1268 London Road
London SW16 4ER
0181 765 7200
http://www.ace.org.uk/contact/

Age Concern Northern Ireland
3 Lower Crescent
Belfast BT7 1NR
01232 235729

Age Concern Cymru
4th Floor
1 Cathedral Road
Cardiff CF1 9SD
01222 371566

Age Concern Scotland
113 Rose Street
Edinburgh EH2 3DT
0131 220 3345

FIVE

The Tin Cup: Money Talk

POINT TO PONDER

The time value of money is the archangel of financial planning.

—Leonard Emmerman, C.P.A.

When we were kids, people who retired were dropouts from life. Women with blue hair and nylons rolled down to their knees gossiped on park benches. Men with huge paunches smoked cigars, hawked phlegm, and listened to Walter Winchell.

We remember Estelle, a colorless, depressed old woman who lived in our neighborhood. Estelle blended into the scenery. She didn't speak, and when she did, no one bothered to listen.

Then Estelle's husband died. The day after the end of her year of mourning, she slipped into the beauty parlor and emerged hours later—hair dyed and permed and eyebrows plucked. She began wearing red lipstick and pearls.

Neighbors laughed. Estelle ignored them and joined a bridge club. She made friends with the sole divorcée in the neighborhood. Then neighbors became annoyed. How dare she be a merry widow at her age? But Estelle didn't seem to care. Between her husband's pension and his Social Security check, she was indulging in joyous independence for the first time in her life. The last we heard of Estelle, she was sailing around the world with a gentleman friend.

COMING TO TERMS WITH THE BIG "R"

In the beginning, of course, we never planned to grow old. It simply wouldn't happen to us! We knew an older couple who were retired. They had a country home, an eight-room condo at the shore, and a *pied-a-terre* in the city. In other words, they were rich.

One day we understood—with a terrible insight that comes in the middle of the night when there's nothing to divert the mind—that soon, we too would be old. We would be poorer than poor. We would be in the street. The angels would weep. We had not saved, and we had not planned, and we were going to be punished big time.

JUDITH'S NIGHTMARE

I'm sitting in the middle of Grand Central Station holding a little tin cup. Everything I own is in a shopping cart. My relatives and friends are running in all directions. They're dressed in furs and expensive suits. Everyone is having a great time, while I sit clutching my tin cup. Some have suitcases or fancy hatboxes, and they're hurrying to catch a train. The dream feels like a 1930s movie, but I'm not Greta Garbo. I'm the Little Match Girl. I call out, but no one can hear. I run after them, but as soon as I step away from my cart, someone steals it. Then everyone is gone, and I'm alone in

Grand Central Station. My only worldly possession is my little cup.

I wake up in a sweat and whisper to Steve, "We have to plan for retirement."

BITING THE BULLET

We called our accountant, Leonard Emmerman—Lenny. We asked if he did retirement planning and if he could help us figure out what to do. He came to our home, and for the cost of a couple of dinners at a good restaurant, Lenny set us on the road to a financially secure retirement. His explanations were straightforward and sensible. He cut through our panic and helped us understand that we have to approach the next financial period of our lives with a fresh eye.

What follows are Lenny's answers to the basic questions we asked.

What are the rock-bottom basics we need to know before we start?

Before anything else, you need to understand the "time value of money." It's very simple. Basically, the time value of money means that the longer you can accumulate money and let the money work for you, the less you need to invest. Let's say you're forty-five and you want to have one hundred dollars by the time you're fifty-five. So you estimate a conservative 7 percent return compounded every year. All you need is fifty-one dollars at age forty-five in order to have one hundred dollars when you get to be fifty-five. If you wait, knowing at forty-five that you want to have one hundred dollars by the time you're fifty-five and do nothing about it, at fifty you suddenly say, "Oh my God, I better do something because I want to have one hundred dollars when I'm fifty-five," you have to start with seventy-one dollars. And, of course, if you wait until you're fifty-five, then you have to find one hundred dollars to have one hundred dollars.

Next, you need to understand that three important factors simply can't be predicted:

Number 1: **Longevity.** You don't know how long you're going to have to spend your money. Obviously, the longer you live, the more money you're going to need or the less you're going to have to spend. I know it sounds simplistic, but it's important to understand. So, how long are you going to live? Typically, people make an optimistic estimate, which is not only human nature, but good financial planning. Barring a war or plague, people are going to be living longer than they think. Take into account your general health and the longevity of your family. The latest U.S. statistics tell us that, on average, men live to 72 and women to 77, but I'm sure you know some people who have passed that mark and are on the road to 90. And then, of course, there's Marie Calamante, who died at the ripe old age of 122. Most of us aren't going to live that long, but to be safe, I like to plan for around thirty years after retirement.

POINT TO PONDER

I've got all the money I'll ever need if I die by four o'clock.

—Henny Youngman

Number 2: **Return on Income.** When you put money aside for retirement, there's no surefire way to predict the return you'll get down the road. In other words, you can't absolutely say for sure how much your savings will grow over the years. A safe, ballpark figure with which to work is 7 percent. It's not pie in the sky. If the economy is booming and your savings exceed that amount, good for you.

Number 3: **Cost of Living.** You can't know for sure the extent to which inflation will diminish your financial assets. No one can accurately predict how much a car is going to cost in twenty years—or a steak or a haircut, for that matter. We can make an educated guess that it will go up by about 3.5 percent, but there's no guarantee it won't go up more.

When you plan for retirement, you have to be flexible. Regardless of how much money you have socked away, you have to deal with the unknowns—that threesome of Longevity, Return on Income, and Inflation.

OKAY—HOW DO WE BEGIN?

First, you need an estimate of your net worth. Then, you have to figure out how much money you're going to have and how much you think you're going to need.

Estimating Your Net Worth

Your net worth is all the money you have left after you subtract everything you owe. You take all the cash you have in savings, in your checking account, your home, your boat, your investments—whatever—and you throw them all into the pot. When you get that number, you deduct from it everything you owe. (See self examination test.)

Your Retirement Income

Basically, you estimate your retirement income by adding your pension funds, your stream of income from the savings you think you'll have—when I speak of savings, I mean IRA accounts, bonds, an annuity, equity funds, etc.—and you add to that your Social Security, work from which you plan to get an income, and some miscellaneous considerations, like the income you may have from the sale of your home.

Pension Plan

Your pension income can come to you two ways:

Defined-Benefit Plan. In this kind of plan, the day you go to work for your employer, he tells you what the deal is with your pension. For example, if you work twenty years, you retire at half pay and every year after that, you'll make another 1.5 percent of your salary. It's set in stone, and the day you start working, you pretty well know what your pension will be. Every year that you get a pay increase you just change the factor in the equation so you can always compute your retirement allowance. Once a year, your employer will give you a statement indicating what your projected retirement benefit will be. That's how you know your private pension plan.

The day you retire, you know what your pension is going to be for the rest of your natural life. It's a fixed benefit. If you're part of that kind of pension plan you don't have to concern yourself with anything about it because it's all being taken care of by your employer. You're not interested in how much money you have in your account, and you're not interested in the rate of return. That's your employer's problem. He promised when you started working for him that he would give you a certain percentage of your salary when you left, and it's his responsibility to have the money put aside for you.

Most organizations are moving away from this type of pension. You can still see it in the uniformed services. Police, firemen and most civil-service jobs still offer defined-benefit plans. There's been no talk of changing pension plans in this sector, but among most private employers, it has virtually disappeared. You don't see it anymore as a new plan, and when companies buy out older employees, typically, they don't give the new employees defined-benefit plans. They provide what's called a defined-contribution plan.

Defined-Contribution Plan. In this kind of plan, from the day you begin the job, no one promises you a fixed-retirement benefit. Instead, the employer promises to put some money into an account for you, and you're also encouraged to put some money into an account for yourself. It may be a 401(k) plan, some sort of profit-sharing plan or an after-tax contribution program. Between you and your employer, you'll make contributions to this plan, and the government lets this money accumulate without taxing it. When you're ready to retire, nobody promises you a retirement benefit. They tell you, "Good luck. Here's your money—now figure out how to make this fit into your retirement equation."

The pot of money we call your pension in the defined-contribution plan will be taken from various sources. It will be a combination of your employer's contribution, your contribution, your IRA savings and whatever else you have when you retire. That's the kind of pension plans people are seeing today. It is up to you to take that money and invest it in a reasonable way so that it yields the kind of return you need in order to live comfortably for the rest of your life.

How do we know what's going on in a defined-contribution plan?

Private pension benefits are typically organized by a company's Human Resources department. They are required by law to give you an annual statement. In general, most companies do it quarterly, although some even do it monthly. The statement indicates the condition of your accounts. Companies that have a defined-contribution plan send you statements that show how much money you have or what your account is worth. So, if you have a profit-sharing plan and, say, a 401(k) plan, you will see the value of each of those accounts and the value of each of the assets you hold.

Savings

Savings Accounts. If you're very careful and save all your money in a savings account that earns 3 percent, you don't have a secure investment. You have a losing investment, because inflation is making your money worth a little less every year.

Stock Equities. It's much smarter to have an investment program that you can anticipate will yield a return greater than the rate of inflation. Between 1926 and 1981, stocks (as measured by Standard & Poor's Index) have basically yielded 10.7 percent before inflation and 7.6 percent adjusted for inflation. Between

1982 and 1996, it's been 15.8 percent a year, and after adjusting for inflation, the rate of growth has been 12 percent.

There are two ways you can look at your savings: You can say that the higher the rate of return, the less money you have to save to reach a goal. Or you can say that the higher the rate of return saving "x" amount of dollars is going to give, the more money you'll have when you retire.

> **POINT TO PONDER**
> With money in your pocket you are wise and handsome, and you sing well too.
> —Yiddish saying

How can we tell if our savings program is solid?
Some benchmarks are commonly accepted for savings programs. If you're saving in anticipation of retirement, a portfolio that consists of at least 80 percent stocks will give you the best shot at growth. The other 20 percent can be fixed-income securities, maybe bond funds, maybe the best-yielding CDs you can buy or a good annuity.

Once you're retired, you have to back off on your investment program because now you're not in the accumulation period. So, now you need a program that will lead you toward a more secure cash flow. In your younger retirement years, that means a portfolio of 60 percent stocks and 40 percent fixed income, and in the mid-retirement years, a 50:50 ratio. In your later retirement years, it may be 30 percent stocks and 70 percent fixed income. You always need an equity portion in your portfolio because it's a hedge against inflation.

What about the risks?

You can't eliminate risk but you can try to manage it. You do that by having an appropriate asset allocation. One school of thought says that an appropriate asset allocation and maintaining that balance during the accumulation period and during the retirement years is as important as what you invest in. In other words, having the right balance is as important as whether you buy Fund A or Fund B.

Social Security

Social Security is the only income I know of right now that is adjusted for inflation. Everything else is just a function of either a fixed pension or a return on your savings.

When you start wondering how much you're entitled to receive when you retire, Social Security makes a form available. It's an Earnings Estimate Form that anyone can get by calling the Social Security Administration. They'll send you an estimate of what you can expect when you retire. You can request an update every year.

Social Security Toll Free Number
1-800-772-1213

Work

When you retire, it doesn't necessarily mean that you stop working entirely. It can mean that you work less, it can mean working at something else, or it can mean that you work for a lower salary. From a financial point of view, work can be anything we need or want to do to supplement our income.

*The dictionary defines "retiring" as Sleep. Cessation of
activities. Quiet individuals are shy and retiring. Baby
boomers have been called many things, but "shy and retiring"
is not among them. We need a new word to describe our later
years. Do we really believe that our sap will suddenly run
dry like a water pipe that's been turned off?*

Home Ownership

When you own your own home, you can sell it, get a pot of money,
and put that into your retirement equation. You can also rent it
and put the rental income into the equation. You can do what people talk about but very few actually act on, which is to get a reverse
mortgage. That means, you get a check from the bank every
month based on the equity in your house. If you do that, you're
betting that you live "x" number of years. If you outlive the reverse
mortgage, you have to deal with losing your home when you may
be frail and advanced in years.

*If you own your own home, pay off your mortgage as soon
as possible. You save a lot on the interest, and you'll have
extra income you can put into savings.*

POINT TO PONDER

A feast is made for laughter, and wine maketh merry:
but money answereth all things.

—The Bible, Ecclesiastes

How can we estimate what we're going to need after we retire?

The best way to anticipate what your expenses will be after you retire is by keeping track of how you spend your money for two years before you retire. It's anxiety provoking for many people to face dead-on the way they spend their money, but it's very helpful. Then you can look at the expenses you won't have after you retire. For example, you aren't going to be paying into Social Security or a pension plan. Your clothing and dry-cleaning bills will probably go down, as well as some other work-related expenses you may have.

On the other hand, you may have new expenses. It's very personal and depends on how you anticipate spending your later years. You also may have additional health costs that you don't have now, and that has to be considered. Finally, you have to factor in inflation of 3 percent.

RETIRING ABROAD

While we're personally not interested in retiring abroad, we have friends for whom this has always been a dream. Here's what one couple said.

➤ We really haven't gone into that next phase of planning ahead, outside of some very general plans. Specifically, we would like to retire to Costa Rica. I see people at work who have actually bought pieces of property, say in North Carolina, and have built homes or drawn up plans or things of that nature. We may say, "Oh, we're going to live in Costa Rica," but we have no concrete plans. We've just begun to think about how we can swing things financially in the next period of our lives, so in a sense, we're really playing catch-up. In our younger years we tended not to look to the future. We kind of had a philosophy that we were going to enjoy life. We took some big trips with the children, and we spent quite a bit of a fortune at one point. Maybe they were not the usual family trips for people in our economic bracket. And we may be paying for that now. We didn't really think, "Oh, we need this kind of a pension plan" or "We're going to save up money for college" the way some people do. So we're just beginning to think of those things.

—*Patricia, age fifty-four; Bob, age fifty-nine*

What's your response to this couple's situation?
It's a pretty common situation. I'd have to know a lot more before I could advise them, but truthfully, most people do not seriously commit to the planning process until they're actually facing retirement. Hopefully, they do commit to the savings process and a good, sound investment program.

What about their plan to retire abroad?
I know you're not asking me about the social or psychological implications. From a purely financial point of view, different areas of the world at different times have different levels of inflation and different values of exchange relevant to the American dollar. If you're looking to the get the biggest bang for your buck, you can move around to places that will, at one time or another, give you the best value for the American dollar. For example, in the 1960s,

Some Americans retired to Spain because the dollar was so strong it drove down the cost of living, but that's changed. You can't assume that fifteen years from now the economic situation in a particular country is going to be what it is now. But if you have an adventurous spirit, and you want to follow the strength of the dollar around, you can move here and there and you will definitely get a bigger bang for your buck.

People who choose to live abroad when they retire have to factor in special expenses. For example, if the couple you quoted ends up flying in from Costa Rica to see their friends and take in a Broadway show every month, or if they buy airline tickets so their grandchildren can visit several times a year, they're going to eat up their savings and may end up actually losing money. If there's a medical condition that requires that one of them see a doctor in the States frequently, then they have to factor in the cost of air travel and maybe even hotel accommodations. It can get more complicated than it seems, and people who want to live abroad need to think about it very carefully.

FINDING A GOOD FINANCIAL PLANNER:

We have a friend who works in a big corporation. The week after she turned fifty, she began to receive phone calls from young men who were eager to help her "make the most of her retirement years." Turning fifty made her a little nervous, so she made an appointment with one.

He was young, charming, earnest and very eager to relate to the older generation she represented ("I play Bob Dylan on my acoustic guitar"). He assured her that if she gave him her money, he would treat it like his own and invest aggressively—because she didn't have much time to fiddle around with slow-moving investments. She needed stocks that would work-work-work. Her modest savings were about to burst into a thousand flowers, each representing a new industry. And this young man would be her loyal gardener, planting the money and fertilizing it with his own manure until it blossomed. . . .

It occurred to her later that with his aggressive approach to money, he might end up a multimillionaire. Then again, he might just end up in the street, tin cup in hand, doing a very bad Dylan imitation.

What's your advice for finding a good financial planner?
Look for someone who is serious about the work and who has credentials. You want a person who has completed a professional program in financial planning. It's best to have a Certified Public Accountant (C.P.A.) who has had additional training as a personal financial specialist. It's a subspecialty, like a doctor who goes for additional training and becomes a gastroenterologist. In the world of accounting, every licensed accountant has to be a college graduate and pass a set of exams to become a C.P.A. After being licensed, he or she can specialize in any of several different areas. A personal financial specialist (P.F.S.) must pass another set of exams, with another set of requirements and a commitment to taking thirty to forty hours of continuing education every year.

You might also choose a certified financial planner (C.F.P.). A C.F.P. does not need a college degree but is required to complete a series of courses that conclude with a qualifying exam. A C.F.P. has had a character check, demonstrated a level of competence in the field, and has had continuing education in his or her area of expertise. The C.P.A./P.F.S. designation comes from the American Institute of Certified Public Accountants, the AICPA, which is a 100-year-old organization.

Stay away from people who are trying to sell you something. Basically, C.P.A.s sell time. They do work, and they charge you for the time. C.P.A.s are fee-based. In the past they weren't allowed to sell, although the laws are changing. In general, you wouldn't look for someone who is interested in selling. You might look for a financial planner who charges by the hour, or if you want some-one to manage your assets, that individual would charge you a percentage, typically one-half to three-quarters of a percent of the assets managed for you. But you wouldn't want the person who is giving you financial advice to be the same person who also sells stocks and mutual funds and insurance policies. It's hard, even for the most honest person, to separate self-interest from client needs.

When you speak to a financial adviser, he/she will ask you to monitor your expenses for a period of time, assess your financial net worth, and try to link it to your longevity, your need for income, and your future living expenses. You can expect that the financial adviser will evaluate this information and come up with a sensible retirement plan.

How much should people put away for retirement?
There is no rule-of-thumb formula. In order to answer that ques-tion, you have to make some reasonable assessment of when you are going to retire, how long you will live, what your cost of living is going to be, and what you can expect from income other than

savings—Social Security and defined-benefit monies. Subtract this sum from the amount you believe you will need to live each month. Once you know what this number is, you can do one of two things. You can figure out how much you need to save every year from the day you first ask that question until the day you retire. Or you can adjust your retirement expectations and plan to live on less.

What happens in the real world is that when you want to retire, the missing factor is going to be the annuity value of your savings—in other words, the amount of money you will have to spend every month over the next thirty years of your life. What's really going to happen with you, with me and with probably most people is that you'll be sixty years old, and you're going to think, well, I'll probably live another thirty years or so. You're going to know what your Social Security is, you're going to know what your regular pension payment is (if anything), and there's going to be a hole. So you'll say to yourself, my spouse and I are getting $25,000 in Social Security, my pension is going to be $6,000 a year, which totals $31,000 a year I can depend on, and I have $600,000 in my savings plan. On that $600,000, you'll make an interest rate assumption. You're not going to be accumulating anymore—that is, no new money will be added to this amount. We're going to assume you'll make 7 percent on the money. Then you know you can take out "x" amount of dollars every year for thirty years—let's say "x" is $30,000.

You'll plug that number into your income, and you can say, "I have $25,000 in Social Security, $6,000 in pension payments, and I can take $30,000 out of my savings every year. So that gives me $60,000." Now you've completed that part of the equation. You know you'll have $60,000 in income, you figure about thirty more years, and you know what? You solved the last part of the equation.

People want to know how much they should save, but most of us don't want to do any of the work. We're not psychologically or emotionally ready to sit down and do budgeting or figure out how long we're going to live, figure out the projected income—it gives many of us a headache to think about it. We just want a real fast answer.

What's a real fast answer?

The fast answer is to maximize your 401(k), maximize your IRA options, maximize your deductible or a work IRA or a conditional IRA, and then have a savings plan that will allow you to save in addition to that.

In the end, if you don't want to do the hard work of figuring out how much you're going to need, you're better off trying to save as much as possible. You're better off overshooting the mark, so that when the time comes and you have to calculate out how much you need, if it turns out you saved too much you can back off on your savings. Or you can choose to leave an estate for your children or leave money to a charity. Or you can have a wild and crazy retirement—or you can do a little of each. Whatever makes you happy. But you know intuitively that you're better off having more money than less. And you know you can't take it with you.

New York State law makes it illegal to bury money in a coffin.

What's the take-home message?

Well, after I give my little spiel, my clients should be thinking one of two things. Either, they're ready to do the work necessary to come to some reasonable conclusion about what their retirement will look like so that they can do what they can to put it into effect. Or they come away thinking, I'm not ready to do this; it seems like a lot of work (and it is). I'm going to have to pay a financial adviser, I'm going to have to prepare self examination tests, I'm going to have to watch my expenses and my income, I'm going to have to think hard about things. I'm not going to do any of that. I'll take Lenny's general advice. I'll just maximize my 401(k), maximize my IRA, see what I can save on the side, and I'll have a good, solid investment program, mostly in stocks. Then, when I'm ready to retire, I'll see where I am, and I'll do the work.

Of course, there's also a third alternative. Somebody might come away from it saying, "This thing is giving me a headache! I want to go on vacation, I'm not worrying about this now." That person is saying "screw the time value of money, I'm not doing this." Once you make that decision, you're kicking the most fundamental, basic principle of capital accumulation right in the teeth. Because the time value of money is the archangel of financial planning.

ONE YEAR LATER . . .

We're looking at our future more realistically. We're never going to have three luxury homes—maybe we can aim for a summer cottage in the mountains. On the other hand, we probably won't be homeless or destitute. Our outlook on the next forty years has changed. We've stopped talking as though it will be an end and have started viewing it as yet another beginning. We've even begun to daydream about what we want to do for the next thirty years of our lives.

SELF EXAMINATION TEST

Your Assets

1. Cash $ Amount

 Money you have on hand   _____

 Money in your checking account _____

 Money in your savings account   _____

 The cash value of your life insurance _____

 Your savings bonds   _____

 Money that's owed you   _____

2. Your Personal Property Est. Current Market Value

 Your car   _____

 Your boat   _____

 Your furs/jewelry   _____

 Your antiques/art   _____

 Other miscellaneous personal property _____

3. Real Estate

 Your home   _____

 Any other properties you own   _____

4. Your Investments

 Stock equities   _____

 Bonds   _____

 Government securities   _____

 Mutual funds   _____

 Other investments   _____

 Equity interest in your own business _____

 Monies owed you by your company even if you leave.

  This includes:

 Pension   _____

 Profit sharing   _____

 Keogh or IRA retirement savings   _____

      Your total assets _____

Your Liabilities

Your Current Bills

    What you owe on your charge accounts   _____

    What you owe on your credit cards   _____

    What you currently owe on your utilities   _____

    What you currently owe on your rent   _____

    Your insurance premiums   _____

    Medical bills/dental bills, etc.   _____

Your Loans

    What you owe on your mortgage   _____

    What you owe on your car   _____

    What you owe on personal loans   _____

    What you owe on installment   _____

    What you owe on your student loans   _____

Taxes you owe   _____

Other liabilities   _____

Your total liabilities   _____

Your Net Worth

Total assets: $_____

          Minus

Total liabilities: $_____

          Equals

Your net worth $_____

Recommended Reading—USA

"Get Real," by Phillip J. Longman, U.S. News & World Report, June 29, 1998, pp. 66–93

Consumers Report Money Book, by Janet Bamford, Jeff Blyskal, Emily Card, Aileen Jacobson, Consumers Report, 1997

You've Earned It, Don't Lose It: Mistakes You Can't Afford to Make When You Retire, by Suze Orman, Linda Mead, Newmarket Press, 1997

Resources

Web sites that offer interactive calculators to help figure out retirement finances:

U.S. News & World Report
www.usnews.com

Fidelity
www.fidelity.com

Web sites relating to Social Security:

Americans discuss Social Security
www.americansdiscuss.org

Issues library on Social Security
Policy.com

Issue briefs on Social Security
www.tcf.org/issue-briefs/social/security/index.html

Social Security Administration
www.ssa.gov

Recommended Reading—The United Kingdom

Pension Fund Excellence: Creating Value for Stakeholders, by Keith P. Ambachtsheer, D. Don Ezra, John Wiley & Sons, 1998

Resources

For a discussion of Stakeholder pensions, pensions fact files and personal finance directory:

www.thismoney.co.uk

For annuity information:

The Annuity Bureau
0171-620-4090

Annuity Direct
0171-598-9393

SIX

Changing Partners

> **POINT TO PONDER**
> Only the fairy tale equates changelessness with happiness . . .
> Only . . . movement, with all its pain, is life.
>
> —Jakob Burckhardt

By the time we reach midlife, each of us has a bittersweet tale or two to tell. We are married—happily or not. We are single. We are divorced. We are widowed, remarried, involved in relationships that are permanent—or not. In short, at middle age we have acquired a "past."

    •⟩ I was thirty-two years old when I married for the first time. I wanted lots of kids. I said six, she said none. I said five or four, she said none. I said three, maybe. . . . Finally, I said two and she said one. She sued for divorce based on cruel and inhumane treatment because I wanted more kids.

—Gary, age fifty-five

❧ I'm scared to death that I'll have a second husband die on me. I don't know if I could make it through another death. I wouldn't mind just meeting someone nice, someone very mellow for companionship, but I don't think I'll ever marry again.

—Rachel, age fifty-nine

❧ My husband died eleven years ago. We met when we were seventeen, and neither one of us wanted to be tied down; we were not into that scene, yet we couldn't let go of each other.

—Natalie, age forty-eight

❧ It was a bad marriage from the beginning. My thinking at the time was that I stayed in it because of my daughter. My wife became an alcoholic, and it was just a mess.

—Howie, age forty-seven

❧ I'm a gay man, and my partner died three years ago. I went through a long period of mourning, and now I'm ready to date again. But I am finding it extremely difficult to meet anyone. On the one hand, when I was younger I had more energy to socialize. I don't meet as many people now. On the other hand, when I do meet someone I might be interested in, that person hasn't shown the slightest interest in me.

Although people tell me I look very young and I'm nice looking, I find I feel practically invisible in social situations.

Peter, age fifty-five

➤ I was twenty-one and had just graduated from college when I was first married, but now I am separated and soon to be divorced. My husband met someone younger. I should have divorced him years ago.

—Pattie, age forty-seven

➤ By the time I got divorced it was as though a weight had been lifted off my shoulders.

—Ed, age forty-six

➤ For all my married life I was secretly involved with another man. Three years ago my husband began a sexual relationship with another woman, and now we're divorcing. In the meantime, the guy I was secretly in love with all these years married someone else.

—Barbara, age forty-one

➤ I was in a terrible first marriage. After eighteen years I finally became strong enough to divorce her. Then I met the love of my life. We became engaged. One month before the wedding, she was diagnosed with pancreatic cancer. We were married for just eight months.

—Barry, age sixty-four

After a long-term relationship ends, either because of irreconcilable differences or death, it takes a long time to heal and to work through the issues that forced the change. You need time to blunt the sharp edges of painful memories and to silence the inner voice that insists you did something terrible, that you could have changed the outcome or controlled something which in reality was outside your control.

You also need to rediscover who you are now that you don't have another person who helps to define you. In this charged period of flux, it's common for people to feel lost and on unfamiliar ground.

With your emotions going haywire, it's tempting to make sense of things by trying to "fix" the external world. Buying a new car, a new wardrobe, changing your hairstyle, or even changing your name are tempting—if temporary—solutions to your emotional confusion. At this stage, it may be most useful to try to find ways to tolerate your uncertainty. Remember, just because you're uncertain doesn't mean you're lost, even if it feels that way sometimes.

WACKY TIME

"Wacky time" is a time of transition between an ending, such as a divorce or the death of a partner, and a new beginning. It is a period of confusion and mourning. Your established identity, be it that of a husband, a wife or a partner is no longer valid because the person who gave you that identity is no longer in the picture. You feel anxious because your emotional equilibrium is out of kilter. You may resort to uncharacteristic or impulsive behavior.

For two years after the breakup of your relationship, you may tend to become involved with people in ways that temporarily mask your self-doubts and unresolved conflicts. You may not exercise great judgment. In other words, you may do some crazy things in pursuit of inner peace during this wacky time.

On my first date after my husband left, I drank as much as I could as fast as I could. I felt very awkward. The guy was appealing, but I felt like I left my personality at home.

—*Pattie, age forty-seven*

When Mel first became divorced, he and a good friend, Ray, who was going through a similar situation, split the cost of an ad in the personal section of a local magazine. They wrote that they were "good daddies" to their children and were looking for a woman with a sense of humor. Neither of them said anything about being handsome or sexy or rich. Just good daddies who liked to laugh.

They received more than four hundred responses, with photographs and detailed biographies. They split the names by tossing them into two hats. Mel calculates that between them they dated some two hundred women before settling down into stable relationships.

You've got to go through wacky time to heal. You may feel like you're spinning out of control, but it's just one of the necessary steps you have to take before you can find a new partner. It's a period of confusion as well as experimentation that's colored by your doubts and insecurities. It's a time to test the waters. Your sense of self is in flux. Don't take any relationship seriously for a while because you can't trust your judgment. Anyone who falls in love with you right now is asking for trouble.

* * *

Judith remembers meeting a lovely man named Robert whose wife had just left him. On their first date, Robert brought Judith flowers. On their second date, he brought a box of her favorite pastries and a bottle of champagne, and on their third, tickets to a sold-out Broadway show. He called between dates and sent sweet little cards thanking her for friendship.

After several months, Judith delicately asked if there was a reason why the relationship never progressed beyond a chaste kiss at the end of the evening. Robert burst into tears. He confessed that he was still madly in love with his wife and that he had been impotent since she left him. Then he blurted out that he was sending cards, flowers and candy to several other women at the same time. He wasn't interested in having a relationship. He was just trying to forget.

After a long-term relationship ends, you may instinctively latch onto the first person you meet and hang on for dear life. Don't do it. The wacky period will recede.

HOLY TERRORS

"Holy terrors" are your personal unrealistic fears and expectations. Like wacky time, they emerge when one phase of life has ended and confusion reigns. Holy terrors represent your anxiety and highlight your vulnerability during this confusing period. Old identities no longer exist and new identities have yet to emerge. Holy terrors will pass.

What's your holy terror?

- Pattie: *When we were first divorced, I was sure I'd be a bag woman, never have sex again, and nobody would ever buy me a gift.*
- Rachel: *One of the reasons I don't want to remarry is that I don't*

want to deal with his children. I don't want to be looked up and down, and I don't want to be accepted or not accepted. I don't want to be judged by people I have no history with.

- John: *After the divorce I woke up every night in a panic because I knew—absolutely knew in my gut—that I was going to lose my job and I wouldn't be able to take care of my kids.*

- Sue: *Larry was the only man I ever went to bed with. I'm scared to death—to put it bluntly—to undress myself in front of another man. I don't know if I can do it.*

Everyone has holy terrors, and they flourish in times of emotional trauma.

Here's how to deal with your holy terror:

- Choose a confidante. Pick someone you trust, someone to whom you can expose the terror to the light of day. Pick someone who won't belittle your fears. Scrutinize your terror with your friend and acknowledge how afraid you are. Examine the terror. Where did it come from? Trying to bury a terror or denying that the fear exists only makes it stronger. Terror feeds on darkness. Shine a light in the dark corners of your mind where the terror lurks.

- Try the following exercise with the help of a good friend who can affirm your strength and capabilities. Take the terror apart step by step:

Exercise to Exorcise a Holy Terror
Terror: Homelessness

How would you become homeless? You'd have to:

- Lose your job.
- Fail to find other employment.
- Lose the support of family and friends.
- Be forced to sell the house and all your possessions.
- Be cast out onto the street.

Talk about the irrational assumptions underlying each of these steps. For example, why would you lose your job? What would you have to do to lose the support of every one of your family members and every one of your friends? Discuss the positive actions you could take at each step to avoid making it happen.

Repeat this exercise until you begin to appreciate your control over the holy terror and can enumerate the resources you have to defeat it.

If you can't shake your terrors or they worsen, think about seeing a cognitive behavioral therapist for short-term treatment. You can get a list of accredited practitioners from your local or state psychological association.

Pick a point person who can provide emotional support.
Choose a person who can help you understand that the feelings you're experiencing are natural. You're not abnormal. He/she can help you realize that you don't have to be overwhelmed by these feelings and that they will change for the better. Most important, this person gives you hope for the future.

The point person can be a psychotherapist, an individual with expertise in a specific area such as finances or legal matters, a peer who is undergoing or has undergone similar experiences, or a friend or family member whom you trust.

   ❖ I got married for the second time when I was forty, after several years of psychotherapy. I was married at nineteen and divorced at twenty-two. I began therapy when I realized that I was frightened of getting involved. I was afraid of men, and I basically viewed relationships like an adolescent until things began to change for me in therapy. I had the outlook of a twelve-year-old or maybe a fifteen-year-old. I was dreamy-eyed. This knight on a white horse was going to come up and rescue me and pay all my bills—that's what I expected when I first got married.

   Today, I wouldn't want somebody to take care of me. That is not the type of a person I am, but I think I was looking for that father figure when I married for the first time.

   I've learned through experience that I don't enjoy being with somebody who is an overly protective kind of person. I've grown enough so I can be independent, and I don't need someone to take care of me.

—Bernice, age forty-four

Psychotherapy can be a useful tool to help you get a handle on important personal issues. It can help you to address specific symptoms you may be having, improve your long-term interpersonal relationships, or manage a crisis.

❧ I was in my late forties when I started my second bache-lorhood, and I was in a terrible hurry. I said "Murray, I want to find a woman, I want to get married and have more kids." Murray said, "Calm down, there's plenty of time."

There I was, panicking because I was in my mid-forties and there was Murray, in his sixties, also divorced, telling me to calm down because there was plenty of time. Every time I had a lousy date, I would call Murray to hear him say, "There's plenty of time." His words were better than a tranquilizer.

—Jerome, age fifty-eight

Empathic individuals who may be experts in areas other than mental health can give you perspective based on their life experi-ence while helping you deal with practical issues.

❧ I grew up believing divorce was the ultimate disgrace. So, you can imagine how desperate I felt when my wife sued for divorce. Two things stopped me from commit-ting suicide: my love for my daughter and the companionship of my friend Stu, who was going through a similar situation.

As the separation process gained momentum and things heated up I would spend evenings with Stu, talking about what we were going through and where we would be when this was all over.

Stu was ahead of me in the process and was just finaliz-ing his divorce, so I had the benefit of his experience.

—Hank, age forty-nine

Friends who have undergone or are undergoing similar traumatic experiences, such as divorce or the death of a spouse, can help you understand what you're going through and reduce your sense of isolation. You can use friends as peer supports. You can also take advantage of support groups that are offered through formal organizations, like churches and local Ys.

Remember, you need time to heal. Give yourself two years to regain your self-confidence, recuperate, and repair the wounds to your self-esteem.

It is natural to be afraid you're going to fail in a relationship again. Regardless of what happened, regardless of whose fault it is, most people harbor a sense that the relationship failed because they weren't *enough—not giving enough, not warm enough, not spontaneous enough, not worldly enough, not tall or thin or rich enough.* . . . It's important to try to differentiate reasonable self-criticism from being unfair or too hard on yourself.

Changing partners is a major life transition. There's a strong possibility you'll become depressed. It's normal to feel sadness, hopelessness, irritability and self-doubt. However, if these feelings seem to be "frozen" inside you, as if they will never go away; if they are accompanied by self-blame, self-criticism, indecisiveness or thoughts of suicide; and if you have physical manifestations such as loss of appetite, sleep disturbance and little interest in doing things, it's more than you should have to bear; it's time to seek professional help.

SELF-REVIEW

Wacky time and holy terrors are irrational. They drain your energy and are counterproductive. Fortunately, they don't last forever. After you've survived your personal wacky time and slain your holy terrors, you may enter a period of self-review. It is a time for introspection, a time to withdraw into yourself for a while and review the relationship that ended. It's a time to get in touch with the confusion you're feeling and to mourn the loss. You may find yourself continually reflecting on the past and mentally rewriting old events in an attempt to change the outcome. You will be sad and you may cry a lot. You may temporarily feel the need to break away from old connections.

Eventually you realize that you can't rewrite history and that you must put this chapter of your life to rest. The sharp edges of pain finally soften and you can begin to think about a new beginning.

But you still have work to do before you can make a commitment to another person. You must first learn how to be alone and live alone.

BEING ALONE

Being alone is an important part of the healing process. It's a state of mind. Being alone is a time to mentally let yourself go, to daydream and figure out what you'd really like to do. It's an intensely creative period. You can allow yourself to fantasize and listen to your dreams. You can't be alone with a partner. You must acknowledge your need to be by yourself. It is a bridge you have to cross by yourself before you can enter a new relationship.

Meditation groups, yoga and tai chi can create a climate
that is conducive to coming to terms with your loss.

Living Alone

Being alone helps you get in touch with your innermost feelings, dreams and wishes. Living alone represents the nuts-and-bolts of surviving the demands of everyday life. Here's how you do it.

- Think about ways you can make yourself comfortable.
- Establish personal rituals.
- Initiate a habit.
- Read a book, watch TV, or call a friend at a specific time each day.
- Create a schedule to make your actions predictable and part of a routine. For example, you might decide that every Tuesday evening you will order in a nice dinner, complete with wine and a fantastic dessert.

The rule of thumb is to spoil yourself. Learn to relish your time alone and to lavish attention on yourself. After a few months, you will start to gain control over your time alone. You'll begin to enjoy it and to relish the space you have. When you're comfortable being alone, you have the power to say, "I don't want to be with this person. I can handle being alone. I'm not driven by the fact that I'm desperately lonely. I don't have to go out with any warm body who walks in the door." Paradoxically, you'll also feel freer to go out and meet people.

Rachel recently lost her husband. These are her observations.

❧ My view of myself changed when I became a widow. I'm stronger than I thought it was. I found that I could depend on myself.

In the beginning you don't know what you're feeling, and you're so busy with paperwork and getting settled, you can't think of anything else. And then I decided to redecorate, and I was busy with paints and carpeting. It was a project that kept me busy, and I was in charge. I was the CEO. I ripped all the drapes off the windows. I ripped out everything I hated, and it was almost like I was saying to my dead husband, "You hurt me so much by dying, so I'm doing this to you. I will show you. You want to drop dead on me, I'm taking everything out." It was wonderful therapy. I told a widow recently, "Go redecorate."

I don't know what a widower would do—men are different. My brother-in-law lost his wife, and it's less than a year later, but he already told me he's looking for someone. I don't think he's redecorating.

When I told him I have no desire for men, he said, "Well, when you get to be seventy or seventy-five don't you want someone to be with? Suppose you get sick?" I said, "If I get sick, I'll handle me." I would never have said that when my husband was alive. I was much more dependent on him than I am on anyone now except myself.

—*Rachel, age fifty-nine*

To recap, you need:

- To learn to become comfortable living alone.
- To address and resolve your holy terrors.
- To identify a point person/persons for emotional support.

After you've gone through these stages, which usually last for two years, you'll have a new sense of yourself and what you have to offer a partner.

NEW BEGINNINGS

You're older now, and you've been through the wars. You've known the thrill of falling in love with someone who was "just too marvelous for words." You've fallen apart and put yourself back together again. Now you're finally ready to make a commitment. And this time, you've learned a thing or two about yourself. You know your limitations and what you need from a partner. You know your strengths. You know what you like about yourself. The second time around, you're looking for someone who can appreciate them. You also have come to a point in your life when you can say, "My job in a relationship isn't to change my partner but to enjoy myself with him/her."

➤ I married the first time because I admired Ella's aggressiveness, her lack of shyness and her "go-get-'em" quality.

She'd meet you, talk to you for five minutes, and want to know how much you earned and how many times a day you made love. Maybe I'm exaggerating a bit. But she could make friends in two minutes. I was very shy and withdrawn, and I was attracted to opposite qualities that made up for my shortcomings. But it didn't work out.

My courtship with Denise was different in that I was just very lucky to meet someone who could appreciate my shyness. She allows me time to myself and doesn't care that I'm not outgoing. She loves me for my qualities, and I love her for hers.

—Jerome, age fifty-eight

❧ I met my current boyfriend in my building. I used to see him in the coffee shop, and he was lonely. He was a very sweet man, but I thought he was less educated than I and that we would never be compatible.

On the day my mother died, I walked back to my apartment, and he happened to be standing in front of the building. He was there, so I told him what happened. We had dinner together, and he helped me with my mother's apartment. He liked me, and I liked him.

We started seeing each other more often. He's a very kind, loving, compassionate man who is emotionally very bright and knows how to have a relationship. I'm teaching him about literature, and he's teaching me things I never knew.

—Suzanne, age fifty-seven

NEW PERSON ON THE BLOCK

What do you do if your adult child doesn't take a cotton to your new love? You've made a judgment that your new partner is a good person. Trust the feeling. Ride out the storm and give support to both your son or daughter and your partner. Listen to your children's feelings—they have to be heard. Use your best judgment, but trust yourself.

❧ Sandy is my son from my first marriage. He was an adolescent when I remarried. In fact, he was the best man at our wedding. He has a limited relationship with the kids from my second marriage. Sebastian was born when Sandy was finishing high school, and Sandy lived with me and my wife in the beginning of the marriage; it was lovely.

The problem was that although Mary was very sweet to him, she didn't really like his values—he was an aspiring rock musician and kind of wild.

Mary went out of her way to be kind and gentle to him, but when Sebastian was born, things changed. Mary became protective of the baby and scared that Sandy would somehow do him harm. It put Sandy's nose right out of joint. He and Mary began to argue. It was a tough period. He'd stay with us, but then he would go back to his mom's for more prolonged periods of time. The year ended quickly, and then he was off to college.

I don't know if I would have done anything differently or if I could give anyone else advice. It's hard to generalize. You have to be understanding and to know that there are going to be good and bad situations and good and bad days.

—*Paul, age sixty*

It's natural that your kids will have something negative to say about your new partner. No child is too old to feel uneasy about changes such as these. It is important to remember that what is good for you may not be good for your adult child, and it doesn't have to be.

When a grown child starts to make trouble when you begin a new relationship, you've got to be clear that it is important to you that everyone works to find a way to make things bearable. The new partner is not there to replace your grown child's father or mother but to be someone for you.

MAY TO DECEMBER

As medical miracles extend our lives and we ride the boom of exercise and healthy living, the phenomenon of May-December relationships becomes commonplace. At the same time, society hasn't quite caught up with the reality of a sixty-five-year-old man wheeling a baby carriage and declaring he is indeed the father and not the grandpa. It's a new world, and our friends and neighbors are pioneers, going where no couple has gone before. They struggle with sending kids to college when they're in their sixties, foregoing personal luxuries out of necessity. They give new meaning to the concept of extending one's professional career beyond the traditional age of retirement. They put to rest the shibboleth of decreasing competence and decreasing sexuality with age. They have reconfigured the family.

His wife died in 1994, and I thought he was very sensitive and sweet but way too old for me. But we began seeing each other as friends—neither of us had any idea where it would lead or what would happen. We just seemed to click, and after a while the age thing didn't matter anymore. It became somebody else's problem if they couldn't handle it.

—Beverly, age fifty-seven

When the kids came along, there was only one important thing for me about the difference in Susan's and my ages. When I look at my kids, when I feel what I feel, when I fill up inside with pride and happiness and joy, to think of these experiences coming so late, brings me a fair amount of sadness. It can be ten times a day or once a day, but, you know, when you have something you didn't have for so many years and then you realize that there are things you're just not going to live to see, things another parent will be able to live to see. . . . It's very sad.

—Barry, age sixty-four

We asked several couples who started families late in life about their retirement plans, and they were a touch wistful. Many had looked forward to retiring and enjoying a period of selfish time not tied up in other commitments.

Older parents are aware that they must help their children through college at an age when they might have been helping themselves. The trade-off, of course, is that they are finding joy and rejuvenation in watching their young children grow.

NONTRADITIONAL FAMILIES

The extended family has come of age. Nowadays, your family can include your ex-spouse, your ex's new mate, your new mate, your new mate's ex and assorted significant others who aren't related by blood or by marriage.

❧ Lynne was my lover for seven years. We broke up because I wanted to have a child and she didn't. I had a son by alternative insemination, and she fell in love with him.

Today, we are no longer involved in a sexual relationship, but Lynne is an actively participating coparent. We have adjacent apartments in a two-family house we bought together and we're raising my son. We are a family in my son's eyes and in the eyes of the community.

We have a very nice family life. I'm forty-nine, she's forty-six, we own a house together, and we're raising a child together. Each of us is going to have to start seeing other people at some point. I would like to do it sooner rather than later.

I know it's going to be very difficult when one of us starts dating somebody new. How am I going to present this to my son?

—Maggie, age forty-nine

Laws written to protect married heterosexual couples don't apply to same-sex couples. They need to take specific legal steps to protect their relationships in the eyes of the law. Important considerations include the legal aspects of having and raising children, domestic partner benefits, state marriage laws, planning for medical emergencies, buying property together, and providing for each other at death. (See Resources.)

✦ My second wife died eight months after our marriage. Her sons by a first marriage lived with me for about a year and then went back to live with their dad. They're now seventeen and fifteen, and I'm like the divorced parent who sees them one weekend a month and a couple of weeks over the summer.

We're very close, but it's an awkward situation. The boys' father is unsuccessful financially, and my present wife and I have become their financial support in a whole bunch of ways.

I'm sixty-four, my wife is thirty-six, and we have two children of our own. We're going to help my stepsons with college, and I put their mother's life insurance money in trust for the boys. I manage the fund, but it's not going to be enough, and we're committed to picking up the slack.

To an outsider, my life is a crazy quilt of extended family and unusual connections. My wife's parents are younger than I am, and my thirty-year-old daughter from my first marriage blames me to this day for things I did wrong when I was her age.

But I wouldn't change my life. Sometimes, when I come home I play with the kids and don't do anything else until they go to sleep. If I have to stay up late, well, at least I've had a chance to see them and spend time with them. It is absolutely delicious. It grounds me and helps me realize that whatever happens, we'll go through whatever we need to in order to survive. It's a wonderful feeling.

—Barry, age sixty-four

When you start a new family, you need time to establish rituals, and time to give everyone a chance to bond. Strangers are coming together with their own values and customs. Even with the best and kindest of intentions, it takes time to blend new family traditions with the old.

At first, you may feel uncomfortable with the newness of this nontraditional family. It may not be everyone's idea of the old-fashioned American family. But with patience eventually, new behavior replaces the old, and it can all work. It's similar to the two-year healing period about which we spoke earlier. This is a time to develop new norms of behavior, new expectations, new roles within the family structure and a whole new family tradition.

At some point, it all comes together, and you all realize you're a family with a unique set of traditions.

A MOTHER'S DAY SAGA

When Judith married Steve she knew that the joint custody arrangement with his ex-wife, Ronnie, might be a problem.

However, everything seemed under control until that first Mother's Day, when nobody knew what to do.

Steve nervously suggested they all go to a local restaurant. The wives were so anxious to be civil and civilized that they totally ignored their daughter, who eventually burst into tears and asked if she had done anything wrong.

The next year, Steve tried to do better. He took Judith and his daughter out for brunch and Ronnie and his daughter out for dinner. The kid loved it, but she had too much ice cream cake and threw up. Steve got terrible heartburn and thought he was having a heart attack. So much for separate but equal.

The third year, they again went to a restaurant as a group, but it nearly ended in a food fight because the mothers were having a terrible argument about summer camp.

Finally, Judith admitted that Mother's Day was giving her nightmares. Steve decided that each woman deserved to have a special day. He designated the second Sunday in May as Birth Mother's Day and the second Sunday in June as Stepmother's Day. The tradition stuck.

Today, their grown daughter brings her boyfriend to both Mother's Day celebrations. The wives have become so comfortable with each other that the entire extended family celebrates both events together.

Recommended Reading

Born to Rebel: Birth Order, Family Dynamics and Creative Lives, by Frank J. Sulloway, Vintage, 1996

Family in Transition, by Arlene S. Skolnick, Jerome H. Skolnick, HarperCollins, 1992

A Legal Guide for Lesbian and Gay Couples (10th ed.) by Hayden Curry (Editor), Denis Clifford, Frederick Hertz, Nolo Press, 1999

Living in a Step Family Without Getting Stepped On, by Kevin Leman, Thomas Nelson Publishing, 1994

Transitions, by William Bridges, Perseus Press, 1980

SEVEN

Love, Sex and All That Jazz

When we were young, sex was a renewable natural resource. We were part of the greatest sexual upheaval since the Kinsey Report. The Pill destroyed our ragtag remnants of Puritan sensibility and opened the floodgates to sexual freedom. Social mores were turned upside down. Young men were . . . well, they were still young men. But now, they could get laid as much as they wanted . . . and how they wanted.

Young women could be fearless. They were suddenly free to explore their sexuality without having to worry about getting pregnant.

It was an outrageous time. The rules disappeared, all bets were off, and we were left to figure out for ourselves what to do in a crazy new world. Our hair was long and our skirts short. We were bearded, bell-bottomed, hedonistic and hell-bent for adventure.

Then we woke up one morning and discovered that Fritz Perl's ditty, "You do your thing and I'll do mine," was no longer the mantra of choice. California dreamin' had given way to watchfulness and obligation. We were overworked, stressed-out, and exhausted. It appeared that the global economic revolution, with its emphasis on mergers and the accumulation of wealth, had won out, hands down, over the Sexual Revolution and its laid-back enjoyment of the moment.

And yet . . . the lure of sweet sexuality continues to sing its siren song. As well it should. Notwithstanding our shifting focus and myriad responsibilities, sexual love remains among the best and most life-affirming of human experiences.

Whatever your lifestyle, please don't forget to practice safe sex.

POINT TO PONDER

Bed is the poor man's opera.

—Italian saying

The authors cannot offer advice on medical conditions that require professional care. Our aim here is to simply address some of the common issues that crop up in our lives that keep us from enjoying our birthright as sexual beings. Men who are experiencing impotence should discuss the problem with their physician. Women who have reached menopause may experience vaginal dryness. Consult your doctor and consider using an over-the-counter vaginal lubricant.

Friends and colleagues have been amazingly forthcoming on a number of issues. We haven't asked them to reveal the particulars of their sexual lives, but over the course of many months, in discussions both casual and intense, some themes kept popping up.

• Everyone complains about a lack of time. It seems that couples in midlife lack the time to take advantage of sexual cues. We don't have time for romance and foreplay, and we don't have time for exciting intrigue. Our adolescent hormones have stopped shrieking, so we don't have the same biological imperatives. In a word, we've grown up, and in doing so, many of us have had to put sex on the back burner. We need to make money, to raise a family, to compete and be successful, to secure a safe retirement, and prepare for a satisfying old age. Sex has a secondary time and a place in our lives, and it's lost its mystique and spontaneity.

> ☙ Gloria and I used to make love. Now, all we do is make money. Funny, isn't it? We're an economic machine. Our income over the last five years has doubled. We're doing very well. We have a house. Our kids are in college. She has a successful career in advertising, and we have all the luxuries in life that we ever wanted. But I'm tired and she's tired. Everybody's tired.
>
> —*Calvin, age forty-five*

• Lots of people complain that they fall into the habit of having sex on a particular day and that they lack spontaneity. They describe their sexual experiences as predictable. We see this problem as just another illustration of a lack of time. We're so overprogrammed that everything gets scheduled—including lovemaking. Sex becomes rushed and hectic, a very small part of a bigger economic plan.

• Women in midlife complain that their partners don't seem to be turned on by them in the same way. They worry that they're not as attractive as they once were.

✦ When I was younger I considered myself an attractive woman. I wasn't a beauty, but I had a nice figure, and men always looked at me. When John and I married—for quite a few years we had a very good sex life. There were times when we didn't communicate or I wasn't ready or he was insensitive or the kids got in the way; we fought about it, but overall I was satisfied. Now that we're in midlife things are a little rocky. I can't help feeling that John doesn't find me attractive anymore.

When I ask him, he denies it or pushes me aside. He doesn't like sex much now. He's either not in the mood or he's just tired or he has too much on his mind. I've started looking at him with a critical eye, and y'know, he's losing his hair and he's got a pot.

—*Harriet, age forty-six*

. . . and men worry about their virility.

✦ When I was younger—in my twenties and early thirties— I really had a ball. I was a single guy, and I must have slept with over four hundred women. It sounds astounding now, looking back on it, but it was fun. I really had fun. Now I'm married, and I guess, what goes around comes around. My wife and I have a good sex life, but it's changed. I need her help in getting going, and this wasn't what it was like when I was younger. It's an embarrassment.

—*Mark, age forty-six*

THE SEXUAL THEATER OF THE ABSURD

At midlife, we are ripe for sexual miscommunication and, surprisingly, a dose of naïveté. When men were in their late teens and early twenties they could engage in a wham-bang-thank-you-ma'am kind of intercourse, having no trouble getting erect or ejaculating. On the other hand, young women needed time to become aroused, and their partner seldom appreciated this.

Now, in midlife, a man faces an extremely stressful period because he is no longer on sexual automatic pilot. It may take him longer to become aroused and maintain an erection. He is susceptible to worrying about performance. Can he get erect? How can he maintain his erection? What does he need to become erect?

A man may be embarrassed to admit to his partner that he's changing. He may compare his sexuality to his reaction time when he was seventeen and assume he's "losing his manhood." It can be quite depressing, and he may lash out at his partner in the false belief that she has failed to keep him young and virile. This change in his response can be very anxiety provoking and inhibit him still further.

A man must come to grips with the realization that his sexual arousal and performance is much more dependent upon direct sexual stimulation from, and engagement with, his partner than ever before. Fantasy alone won't always work.

Meanwhile, a woman may internalize these feelings and begin to see herself as sexually unattractive and view her partner's lack of immediate response as a rejection. She may interpret his performance anxiety as a comment on her sexuality as well as physical attractiveness. Because of a lack of understanding on both sides, the anger flows, and everyone is unhappy and sexually frustrated.

And yet, the midlife years offer great potential for a reinvigorated sex life. There's a new equity between the sexes, and men and women may finally be in sync in terms of sexual timing.

In fact, women may find themselves leading their partner more than they did when they were younger and enjoying sex more than they did when their partner set the pace.

Several factors influence a heterosexual woman's sexual appetite in her middle years. It may take years for a woman to become comfortable with her sexuality. She may have buried it beneath a mountain of responsibilities and family obligations. Her partner may have been insensitive or simply ignorant of female sexuality, and she may have been too embarrassed or shy to discuss her needs. She may have feared an unwanted pregnancy. Her living arrangement may have offered limited privacy, and she may have been worried that her children might hear her during sex or walk in at an inopportune moment. Because a woman's sexuality usually requires a slow buildup to reach orgasm, it may have been expedient for her to satisfy her mate and put her own sexual satisfaction on the back burner.

Then she enters midlife and everything changes. Her children grow up, her partner slows down sexually, and she begins to go through menopause. Things seem to be turned upside down. We will not discuss menopause here except to say that many options exist for women today to minimize the effects of the decrease in estrogen. If you think you have begun to go through menopause, visit your gynecologist.

As well as physical changes, psychological changes occur when a woman no longer has children living in the house. She may have a close, loving and supportive relationship with each of her children, but when offspring move out a woman is no longer responsible for them on a day-to-day basis. Her home becomes truly private.

A woman in midlife is less fearful about sex. She is more mature, more sophisticated and more knowledgeable than she was when she was young. She is also more creative. She is more likely to tell her partner what pleases her and to listen to his sexual fantasies with an open mind. She is freer to be curious, playful and more experimental than she could be when she had children in the next room. She may have more discretionary income with which to buy sexy lingerie or a weekend getaway.

We can debunk the myths about midlife marking the end of sexual love by accepting our changing bodies and taking advantage of the glorious sensual pleasure that life has to offer.

As with so much else that happens in midlife, the sex lives of men and women are undergoing major transitions. We believe that at midlife, couples have the potential for sexual renewal and sensual delights.

If you feel overwhelmed by sexual doubts and your doctor has ruled out any physical illnesses, you and your partner might want to consider consulting a licensed sex therapist.

A FEW WHIMSICAL, OUTRAGEOUS, TOTALLY FOOLISH AND UNABASHEDLY ROMANTIC SUGGESTIONS RESPECTFULLY SUBMITTED FOR YOUR CONSIDERATION

Making Time

Unschedule your lovemaking

- Make love in the morning.
- Make a date for a quiet rendezvous at lunchtime.
- Have a little foreplay before going out for the evening to get you excited and in the mood for the main attraction when you get home.
- If you have the right setup, invite your partner to the office at lunch or after hours. Lock the door. Tell your secretary to hold all calls. Make love on the desk, the floor, the sofa. (Make sure the cleaning people don't barge in.)

POINT TO PONDER

It doesn't matter what you do in the bedroom, as long as you don't do it in the streets and frighten the horses.

—Mrs. Patrick Campbell

Create a secret interlude.

Meet in a hotel lobby and reserve a room for an entire afternoon of unstructured delight.

- Instructions for men: Wear dark glasses. Bring champagne and two glasses in your attache case. Bring good-smelling oil with which to massage your partner.
- Instructions for women: Wear a raincoat and sexy under-wear—or nothing—underneath. Titillate your partner. Wear a wig and dark glasses.

Have a brief sexual encounter

- Fondle in an elevator.
- Neck in a staircase.
- Get hot in a car.
- Grope each other at the movies.
- If you can afford to splurge, rent a limo for a couple of hours, drive to nowhere and back. Give the driver something to talk about.
- Cancel a business engagement and come home to make love instead.

POINT TO PONDER

Each is pleasured in the act of pleasuring the other.

—Anonymous

Rediscovering Sexual Playfulness

Tell everyone you're out of town for the weekend. Then . . .

• Create a sexy mood in your bedroom. Use incense, candles, silk sheets, dim lights, music to create a different ambience. Turn off the telephone and TV. Hide the piles of work you have stashed in the corner or on your desk.

• Rent a romantic old movie to get you in the mood.

• Rent a couple of X-rated movies to get you going.

• Buy foods that say "Gone Fishing." For some people it's oysters and champagne; for others, mangoes and papayas; and for some, pizza and beer says it all.

• Some restaurants will deliver Sunday breakfast in bed. Order in advance.

• Spend the weekend relaxing in bed, teasing and pleasuring each other.

• Don't forget to stock up on massage oils, movies, books, erotica and anything else that makes the two of you happy.

Watch an erotic movie with your clothes on.

Don't touch and don't undress. After it's over, undress each other.

Play Scrabble.

Each time you get points, you also get one erotic favor of choice. The aim is to finish the game without having an orgasm. Save that for the postgame party.

Take turns reading to each other . . . and we don't mean
The Wall Street Journal.

An Idiosyncratic List of Erotic Reading Material

Slow Hand: Women Writing Erotica, edited by Michele Slung
Under the Roofs of Paris, by Henry Miller
Herotica, edited by Suzie Bright
Pleasures, by Lonnie Barbach
The Black Book, by Lawrence Durrell
Delta of Venus, by Anais Nin

POINT TO PONDER
License my roving hands, and let them go,
Before, behind, between, above, below.

—John Donne
"To His Mistress Going to Bed"

Giggling Can Be Sexy

- Share a shower and lather each other *real slowly.*
  (You might want to use baby soap—commercial brands can
  sting delicate tissues.)
- Have a water pistol fight in your underwear or T-shirts. It's
  messy but a lot of fun, and it's sexy.
- Spend an afternoon in a sex shop. Go incognito! Wear
  dark glasses, wear a wig, paste on a mustache or beard.
  You'll both look hysterically funny, have a wonderful time,

and unless you wear a name tag, no one will know who you are.

- Women: Use depilatory to change the way your pubic area looks.
- Men: Wear a jockstrap to bed.
- Pretend you've been hired to please your partner sexually. You don't know what this person likes or desires. You need to find out and then act accordingly.
- Do a striptease for each other.
- Make love in front of a mirror.
- Write a sexy, hot note on e-mail.
- Buy each other sex toys.

POINT TO PONDER

If God had intended us not to masturbate,
He would have made our arms shorter.

—George Carlin

What self-respecting authors of a chapter devoted to sex can let the opportunity pass to tell you what you already know: Masturbation is good for you.

- Masturbate to prime the pump.
- Masturbate when you want to do some healthy fantasizing.
- It's not just for kids—it never was.
- Enjoy yourself.

GETTING BACK TO BASICS

Someone made the comment that we are turned on by strangers because we don't know them.

Yet the truth is that each of us is sexually multifaceted. We are fascinating, inscrutable and veiled in mystery. We've quite simply been sabotaged by the stresses and the sameness of our daily lives. We need to relearn how to reveal ourselves to our partner in new ways.

Couples can help each other embark on an exciting, erotic journey of discovery. The intimate sexual exposure we allow ourselves with a trusted partner can be as explosive and erotically liberating as anything we've experienced in the past twenty-five years of our lives.

Recommended Reading

Extraordinary Sex Now: A Couple's Guide to Intimacy, by Dr. Sandra R. Scantling

Mars and Venus in the Bedroom, by John Gray, HarperCollins, 1997

Sex Over 40, by Saul H. Rosenthal, M.D., Jeremy P. Tarcher, 1987

The New Joy of Sex, by Alex Comfort, Simon & Schuster, 1998

Yesterday, Today and Tomorrow

Judith will never dance with Fred Astaire.

When she was nine, she wrapped a cabbage rose bathrobe tightly around her skinny torso and became Ginger Rogers. She twirled and vamped and knocked herself out. The family beamed and applauded. Fred was there in spirit, but everyone just knew that in time her talent would twirl her into his arms and into the hearts of the American people. . . .

Guess what? Fred's dead, and Judith is a fifty-four-year-old woman with bad knees.

At midlife we become equal parts of memory, pleasure and remorse. Our pride in life achievements is mingled with regret over things we will never possess and heights we will never reach.

When you were a kid, did you want to be a circus performer? A bank president? A mommy? A writer? All of the above? Did you grow out of your dreams, or were they deferred indefinitely, waiting for the right time, until they faded into memory?

Steve wanted to be a radar technician and track airplanes, until his guidance counselor suggested he train to be a car mechanic instead. Today, instead of keeping planes on course, Steve's job enables him to give people the emotional compass they need to navigate their lives.

Can we regain our footing on the road we abandoned years ago? Is it possible to reconnoiter and, with the hindsight of years, do it over again, only this time differently?

Some roads can never be rediscovered. You lose your virginity once. You have one fleeting season to be sixteen in Paris in the spring. Decisions have a way of being made and life lived in peculiar ways. And some dreams are lovely only because they can never be realized. They live where they belong—in our glorious fantasies.

THE AUTHORS FANTASIZE

We dream of opening a restaurant. We will serve wonderful soup and homemade bread. We, in turn, will receive the timeless pleasures of friendship. A kind of "Cheers" without beer, an update on the parable of the loaves and fishes. Our soup pot will never be empty and our oven never cold.

Don't drop by just yet, though, because neither of us has ever worked in a restaurant. Not even for a single day. Neither do we have any intention of engaging in the back-breaking, labor-intensive work that comes with owning one. And, in case you're wondering, neither of us knows how to bake bread.

Still, reality doesn't keep Steve from occasionally looking up from his newspaper and saying in a dreamy voice, "Y'know what I'd really love to do . . ."

We must give ourselves credit for the struggles in which we do engage and not belittle the effort or the worthiness of the task. Sometimes our job in life is to dream. At other times, we begin to navigate our dreams so they can enter the real world and become part of the lives we've chosen. Then there are periods of time when we work on the decision we've made, struggle to meet the challenge, to rise to the task, to overcome our fears. We wouldn't make light of an eighteen-year-old's conflict over whether to attend college or join the army or take a year off from school to go on a wonderful adventure. Why belittle our own dreams?

There are lots of reasons why people change their life's direction in midlife: financial, personal, circumstantial. Some of the people to whom we spoke seemed to be made of whole cloth. They were born knowing what they wanted from life and went on to pursue the dream. For many however, life has been a series of compromises, disappointments and reevaluations. Midlife is a time when we once again reevaluate the course we have taken. The world has changed since we were young, and so have we. Midlife is a time to reassess where we are and what we want for the next thirty-five years.

We asked friends what they wanted from life as kids and what they'd like now, and we were amazed by some of the responses. People we thought we knew revealed wonderful new aspects of themselves.

Michele:

I wanted to be a lawyer, but my parents, particularly my mother, encouraged me to be a teacher. They thought it was the best option for a girl. If my husband died, I could support myself.

After I retire, I don't know what I'll do. I've thought of everything from opening a bookstore to starting some kind of consulting business to going for a master's degree in history. I feel like I've been in school for my entire life. I'd like to do something different.

Peter:

As a kid, I wanted to be a firefighter. Then, around the age of fifteen things became muddled, because given my academic standing and my family, I had to choose an academic career. If I had to do it over, I would have become a firefighter—at least for a while.

In the near future, I plan to relocate to Guatemala. While I am open to using my skills as a psychologist and my managerial skills to possibly volunteer in Guatemala, I want to look into other possibilities, such as opening a business. But whatever I do, in Guatemala or elsewhere, what I want to do is something creative. I had no passion about the career I was in. Do I have a plan to achieve these goals? Well, plan one is to do something that I have wanted to do for at least twenty years and that is to immerse myself in a completely different culture. And while I'm there, for at least maybe a year, to really look around and see if there is something I find that I think I want to spend time and energy on over the years.

Beverly:

One thing I always loved was art. Probably that was because I used to paint with my mother when I was a kid. I wanted to be an artist when I grew up, but then as I became a teenager I also wanted to be a parent, and it didn't happen in my life that I became a parent, but I did become a teacher.

I find I have other needs now. I'm going to continue teaching in a different environment when I teach ESL for adults. But I also want to explore the parts of myself that I had to put aside when I was teaching because I had so little time for myself.

I would like to study art again and paint. I've always wanted to continue with my study of music that I began when I was a kid. I'd also like to write some. I think what I want is to get back into my creative self.

Natalie:

The only thing I wanted to be when I was a kid was a butcher. It looked like fun. I think it was expected that I would get married and have kids, but beyond that it was a blue-collar area and the highest most women I knew aspired to was being a secretary.

What I really want to do is go back to what I was doing before what I'm doing now, which was writing.

After leaving graduate school, I decided that I wanted to be a writer and began seriously writing immediately, and I had my first novel published in 1983. My novel was actually nominated as one of the best novels of the year by the American Book Award. And at that point, I really figured "Okay, I just keep doing this" and started a second book, which was a nonfiction book on psychiatry. But then my husband died, and I needed to make a living, so I kind of stumbled into the job I have. I'm ready to go back. My kids are out of college, and I'm ready to go back to full-time writing.

Anita:

I hope to keep doing what I'm doing for many years to come. I want to remain active professionally, travel, and enjoy the good friends I've made over the years.

Howie:

I always wanted to change the world. My plan was to save my money so I could buy a small airplane—kind of like Sky King. When I was growing up, Italy was at war with Trieste. My fantasy was that I would load my plane with food and Snickers bars and drop them over Trieste so the kids would have food. When I got older, I wanted to enroll in the Peace Corps, but I ended up going into my father's business. It's been really successful, and I'm about ready to sell it and retire. I'm divorced, and my kids are nearly grown. I think that I may finally be able to do what I always wanted—which is join the Peace Corps.

Patricia:

When I was in college my family expected that I would marry and never have to work. I guess they thought I'd be a traditional housewife and maybe paint a little on the side because I've always had an artistic bent. I only stayed married a short time, and after the divorce, my father hired me to work in his company. I worked my way up—being the boss's daughter got me in the door, but I worked very hard.

Since my father sold his business, I've been trying to find work that would make me happy. I recently started working in an art gallery, and I love it. I plan to take courses in art appraisal and further my career. I hope that in the years to come, I can finally come into my own as a professional in the arts.

Esther:

I want to keep going on the path I carved for myself years ago—developing my work, my relationship with my daughter, my guy, my mind, my humor.

Maggie:

I always wanted to be a writer. And I remember writing my first book. I was eight, and I came into possession of a little notebook, one of those little tiny ones with the spiral on top. And I thought, "This is wonderful, I'll write a book." And I remember sitting down to write the book and encountering question number one: Do I make up my own story or should I use somebody else's story? And at that point, I chose somebody else's story.

Now I'm verging on fifty. I'm working on the fourth novel I've attempted. I never really finished the three preceding ones. But I felt very powerfully that I must not turn fifty without having written a book that I had really given my all to and that thoroughly expressed my view of life.

And now the novel has been accepted as a thesis in the master's degree program in creative writing at San Francisco State University, and I am polishing up the novel so I can send it out to agents before I hit fifty. I need to feel comfortable approaching this milestone, knowing I kept faith with myself.

A friend who lives in a seaside community tells us that sometimes in winter the bay freezes over and becomes a sheet of ice. But in the night she hears groans as the water beneath the icy crust forces its way up against the still surface. In the morning the bay is fissured like a huge puzzle. It is her metaphor for life at fifty—a life she tries to keep placid but one that nevertheless surges with emotions and desires that break through to the surface. It's a metaphor we have taken to heart.

Midlife is a wild, messy, wonderful time—chaotic and fraught with fears but at the same time strangely exhilarating. We wanted to share our observations and our stories as we stumble through.

A door we thought had closed forever is beginning to creak open, and if we peer through the crack we can vaguely make out the outlines of the future. And so, we leave you with the most optimistic word we know: Tomorrow.

Exercise 1

1. List five life experiences that helped you to be the person you are today.

2. List five life choices you made that were instrumental in making you the person you are today. (It's okay if 1 and 2 overlap. It's okay if they don't.)

3. List your personal "roads not taken"—as many as you want.

4. Do any (or all) of these roads still beckon?

5. Do you prefer your "road not taken" to remain in the realm of delicious fantasy?

6. Is your "road not taken" a potentially do-able adventure? Does it still beckon?

7. If it isn't do-able, but you're still obsessed, is there anything you can do to make it so?

Exercise 2

1. What was your life goal/fantasy when you were a teenager?

2. What would you like to salvage from those dreams?

3. What were your life goals/fantasies at thirty?

4. At forty?

5. What's your fantasy for the next thirty years of life?

6. What would you need to realize that dream?